KEYS TO BUYING AND SELLING A BUSINESS

Steven A. Fox
Attorney-at-Law, LL.M., CPA
West Palm Beach, Florida

BARRON'S

All inquiries should be addressed to:
Barron's Educational Series, Inc.
250 Wireless Boulevard
Hauppauge, New York 11788

Library of Congress Catalog Card No. 91-2531

International Standard Book No. 0-8120-4430-4

Library of Congress Cataloging-in-Publication Data
Fox, Steven A.
    Keys to buying and selling a business / Steven A. Fox.
      p. cm.
    Includes index.
    ISBN 0-8120-4430-4
    1. Small business—Purchasing—Law and legislation—
United States. 2. Small business—Finance—Law and
legislation—United States.
    I. Title.
KF1659.F69   1991
346.73'0652—dc20
[347.306652]   91-2531
                                CIP

PRINTED IN THE UNITED STATES OF AMERICA
6 7 8 9 0 5500 9 8 7 6 5 4 3 2

CONTENTS

1

INTRODUCTION

Deciding to buy or sell a business is a milestone for any entrepreneur, such a decision clearly changes your life. Whether you're an employee risking it all to buy a business or a business owner ready to sell your company and retire, the transaction must be carefully analyzed.

Making the decision itself is difficult. Family, friends, professional advisers, and just about everybody else will focus on what can go wrong. A buyer may wonder if the seller is lying about the business's sales record; a seller may wonder if the buyer really wants to buy or is gathering information for the competition, or is even from the IRS.

This book focuses on "due diligence," which is the investigative effort involved in checking out the other side's story. Although much information, such as the existence of tax liens is "on the record" and can be easily verified, other information, such as your potential buyer or seller's integrity is harder to come by, although important. Although this book cannot obtain the information for you, it can help you apply that information, both quantitative and qualitative, in the decision-making process.

This book is not intended to serve as a substitute for legal, tax, or other advice that you might obtain from qualified advisers familiar with your individual needs and your jurisdiction's requirements. Rather, it is designed to frame the issues in a way that helps you make the best use of your time with any advisers you engage. This book will not make you an instant expert, but it will provide a good deal of practical information on issues of particular relevance to your situation.

2

ARE YOU AN ENTREPRENEUR?

This key and the three that follow focus on the "buy" side of the transaction. Clearly, the decision to give up your job and a steady salary for the hazards of self-employment and an all-consuming emotional and financial commitment to a business should not be taken lightly. Just because you dislike your current position does not mean that you are ready financially and otherwise for self-employment. This key will help you decide whether you are cut out for self-employment.

Self-employment has a number of benefits. First, owning your own business offers a potentially greater income stream than is generally available to an employee. Many people work hard for years but never get the right raises, promotions, or breaks because of office politics or other considerations. For self-employed people, there is usually a correlation between hard work and economic return. Second, being self-employed offers greater independence and stability than working for others. Third, working in a small business enables you to engage in many satisfying activities not available to an employee because you are in control of your own time and are free to spend it as you see fit.

Even if you feel that you are cut out for self-employment you will not necessarily make it on your own. Statistics show that about 65 percent of all new businesses fail within five years of inception. Although a substantial number of these failures are attributable to poor market conditions and similar external factors, a large number of failures are attributable to a failure in the owner-manager. Therefore, it is useful to describe those qualities associated with the successful entrepreneur.

First, although inherently individualistic, such people are leaders who are able to direct and control others, and they often do not fit in well in traditional hierarchical, structured environments. They tend to have considerable self-confidence, are well-organized, and enjoy taking on new problems and identifying solutions. They can make decisions and stick to them and they know when to admit mistakes and how to make the necessary corrections. They are practical and have reasonable expectations about what they, their employees, and others can accomplish. They are emotionally stable, tend to be in good health, and have good family relationships. Overall, they have a long-range vision of what can be accomplished, both short- and long-term.

The successful entrepreneur should also possess proven skills in as many of the following as possible: management, sales, marketing, retailing, public relations, advertising, merchandising, accounting/finance, cost control, and inventory control. Although you can hire employees and consultants who have these skills, the more knowledgeable you are in these areas, the greater your likelihood of success and the fewer the number of mistakes you will make during the learning phase.

3

BUYING AN EXISTING BUSINESS VS. STARTING FROM SCRATCH

Assuming that you do have the necessary interest and skills to make it in self-employment, one of your first decisions is whether to buy an existing business or to start one from scratch. There are pros and cons associated with each.

If you start a business from scratch, you can choose the best location available, rather than be stuck with the current location of the business. A less obvious advantage of starting anew is that you can make the most efficient use of modern equipment, design, and energy sources, including provisions for future growth in capacity, rather than to try to make changes on an as-needed basis. When you start a business from scratch, you can be innovative in naming the business and in your marketing and pricing strategies; you may be locked into those already in use with an existing business.

Starting from scratch does have some negatives. It will take some time to put together a financing package, especially if the entrepreneur is an unknown quantity. It will take additional time to get the business ready for opening and still more time to build up a customer and supplier base. Further, unlike the purchase of an existing business, where there is a definite price involved, it is difficult to measure accurately the total costs for starting a new business. Often the projections are substantially understated. In fact, the unknowns—from whether the goods or services will be accepted by consumers to whether credit will be extended by vendors—can be overwhelming.

Overall, the risk of failure tends to be higher with startups than with purchases of existing business, especially of franchises. In any given year, fewer than 5 percent of all franchised business are discontinued. Part of the reason for this is that generally it costs more to start a new business and to bring it up to a profitable sales level than to buy a going concern.

A big advantage of buying an existing business is that as a rule, it is easier to obtain financing, since there is a proven track record on which to base a loan, existing assets can be used as collateral for the loan, and a reporting system is in place and operated by experienced employees. Since the business is already operating, it should be possible to assess future potential with greater accuracy and the vendor and customer base will be already established, all of which should enable the business to realize an immediate return on the investment without a protracted period of uncertainty. Of course, if the business has been run by an owner-manager, the loss of that manager may lead to a substantial disruption in operations. This problem can be ameliorated by negotiating a continuing relationship with the seller-owner for a specified period of time, perhaps six months, after closing takes place (see Key 8).

Buying an existing business does have some disadvantages. The buyer will likely be locked into the existing policies and practices of the former owner. For example, if the seller has consistently underpriced the business's product or service, it may be difficult for the new owner to increase the price immediately. The buyer will also be locked into the business's present location and traffic patterns, at least for the near term, even if they are less than ideal. This means that if parking is poor and zoning restrictions make it difficult to increase the parking facilities, the owner will face a problem without a realistic solution.

The new owner will inherit not only the customer/supplier base but the current employees, some of whom may have grown lazy. It may be expensive to make repairs to the business, and the prior owner, knowing that he intends to sell, may have allowed the business to run down. There may be competition the buyer is not aware of, which may be the real reason, if not the expressed reason, for the sale. For example, the owner of a liquor store may know that a discounter will soon open in the area.

In any case, the new owner will need time to gain acceptance by the employees, because of their loyalty to the prior owner and their inherent resistance to change. Sales levels, profit margins, and other financial indicators of success frequently go down after an ownership change because of employee resistance to the new owner. Although there is no sure way to eliminate the risks the entrepreneur will face, it is possible to minimize them; for many, the best way to do this is to buy a well-run business with a proven, documented, and maintainable track record.

4

THE FRANCHISE OPTION

This key considers a third possibility for the budding entrepreneur—buying a franchise either directly from a franchisor or from a current franchisee. In a franchise relationship, one party, the franchisor, licenses another, the franchisee, to sell the franchisor's goods or services in a particular location for a certain period. The franchisee ordinarily pays a fee for this privilege plus a royalty on gross sales. The term franchise refers not only to the right to sell a particular good or service but to the place in which the franchisee exercises that right.

Broadly speaking, there are two types of franchising. The first type is product and trade name franchising, such as an automobile dealership, in which the franchisee concentrates on one product line. The second type is business-format franchising, which involves an ongoing relationship between franchisor and franchisee, a standardized method of doing business, and an image that is attached to the goods or services. A common example is a fast-food franchise. This type presently represents about ¾ of all franchised businesses in the U.S.

There are various subgroups within these broad categories. In a unit franchise, for example, the owner has the right to open one outlet at a specified location or within a specified territory, while in an area development franchise, the owner has the right to open outlets within a specific territory. In a master franchise, the owner must open a certain number of units in a certain geographic area and within a certain amount of time. The franchisee has the right to sell franchises within an exclusive territory and must satisfy a minimum quota for franchise sales or development. Conversion franchising seeks to convert independently-owned outlets into the system.

A franchise offers numerous advantages to both franchisor and franchisee. For the franchisor who has developed a successful product or business format, franchising offers an ideal way to duplicate a business concept in many geographic locations without investing the capital, time, and effort required to create company-owned stores or outlets. The franchisee puts his or her own money on the line and will probably be more dedicated to the effort than an employee without that investment. Although the franchisor receives a relatively low initial fee from the franchisee, often just enough to cover marketing and training costs, the franchisor will eventually get a fair return from ongoing royalties as well as from the franchisee's continuing purchases of supplies or products.

Since the franchisor's success depends on the franchisee's success, the franchisor naturally tries to select the best franchisees. Unfortunately, though, the franchisor has less control over a franchisee than over a company store. Further, federal and state disclosure requirements, as discussed below, make franchising a regulatory minefield.

Franchising takes some of the risks out of going into business and reduces the start-up cost faced by the entrepreneur. A franchise enables a person to get set up in a business with a relatively small capital investment. Although relatively few franchisors provide financing, the franchisor may agree to guarantee a bank loan, and this may convince a bank to make a loan or grant more favorable terms. The franchisee, who acquires a proven format to work with and receives training as well as ongoing assistance from the franchisor, also benefits from the franchisor's name, management expertise, advertising, and cooperative buying power.

Franchising has its negatives too. The franchisee has only limited territorial rights, thereby limiting the potential for growth, is subject to rigid franchising fees and sales quotas, and may have a restricted source of supply.

Further, the franchisee "owns" the franchise only during the franchise period, which may or may not be subject to renewal, and any effort to transfer the franchise may be fraught with problems. In fact, some franchisors impose a hefty franchise fee for the transfer of an existing franchise. Overall, if you want to be free to innovate, to make an operation truly distinctive, to add new product lines, if you object to paying franchising fees and to purchasing products or services from a franchisor rather than from an independent vendor—and if you think that you can make it on your own without help from an experienced organization—then franchising may not be for you.

How do you decide on the best franchise for you? In addition to the national and local newspapers and magazines that describe franchise opportunities in the business opportunities section, there are periodicals that specialize in the topic. Frequently, there is an "800" number to call for those who want more information about the franchise. There are government publications on the subject as well as franchise brokers who offer information on different franchise investments. You should investigate every franchisor that seems appealing. You will receive a marketing kit containing descriptive information about the franchise and be asked to complete an application. After you return the completed application, the franchisor will run a background check on you, including your credit history.

You will receive a lot of information immediately from the franchisors and should eliminate from consideration those that aren't feasible. To do this, consider the history of the franchisor, the required investment, the royalty levels (which may include a separate royalty to contribute to an advertising trust fund), the training offered, the franchisor's advertising program, and any geographic restrictions that apply. Early on, you should try to obtain a list of franchisees convenient to you and speak with as many as possible.

Once you have narrowed the franchisor list down to a few prospects, review the documents provided as thoroughly as possible with your advisers. By law, the franchisor must furnish you with a full disclosure statement at least ten days before a contract is executed or before any money is paid, whichever comes first. Failure to comply with this regulation constitutes an unfair trade practice under Section 5 of the Federal Trade Commission (FTC) Act.

Under the so-called FTC Rule, the disclosure statement must provide the following information: identifying information; business experience of the franchisor's directors and executive officers; business experience of the franchisor; litigation and bankruptcy history; description of the franchise; initial and recurring funds required to be paid by a franchisee; affiliated persons with whom the franchisee is required to do business; any obligations to purchase; revenues to be received by the franchisor; financing arrangements; restrictions on the way the franchisee conducts business; personal participation required of the franchisee; policies governing termination, cancellation, and renewal of the franchise; certain statistical information; rules for site selection; training programs; any public figure involvement in the franchises; and financial information.

You have other rights too. You have the right to receive a sample copy of the franchisor's agreement at the time you receive the disclosure statement and to receive the final agreement at least five business days before you are asked to sign it. You have the right to receive an earnings claim document any time the franchise makes a statement, whether verbal or written, as to what return a buyer may expect on his investment and this document must be updated every 90 days. You have the right to receive any refunds promised by the franchisor subject to any disclosed limitations. In addition, certain states afford the franchisee additional rights. The states are permitted to impose standards stricter than the FTC requirements, but the FTC standards apply if a state's standards are less stringent.

As part of your due diligence effort in checking out the franchisor, you should investigate the franchisor's reputation with the local Better Business Bureau, conduct a credit investigation on the company involved, and try to speak to customers, employees, suppliers, and others who have had dealings with the franchisor. Once you have completed your investigation, you need to investigate the merits of a particular location (the financial strength of the franchisor may help in finding a prime site). Your attorney should be actively involved in assessing this information and should help you understand the franchise agreement. The agreement normally contains provisions relating to payments, the franchise grant (in area and duration), training, royalties, standards and uniformity in operation, insurance indemnification, taxes, renewal rights, assignment or transfer of the franchise, any limitations imposed on the franchisee, and a host of other clauses. For example, the potential franchisee should be sure to understand how disputes between the franchisor and franchisee will be settled and any provisions that enable a franchisor to buy back the franchise because the franchisee is successful or because the franchisor has sold out to a larger company that wants to take over the franchise. An investment in legal fees at this point should prove to be money well spent.

5

THE ACQUISITION PROCESS: THE BUYER'S VIEW

This key presents an overview of the process of acquiring a company from the standpoint of the buyer. First, you must develop a set of criteria for evaluating possible acquisitions. Second, you must find potential acquisitions that meet those criteria and investigate them. Third, you must zero in on a target company. Fourth, you must negotiate the purchase, with the assistance of your advisers. Fifth, you must obtain financing for the purchase. Sixth, you must work out the final details of the transaction.

The acquisition criteria are crucial, since they will be used to rank various prospects. Mergers-and-acquisitions specialists need such criteria to help them locate good matches, and so does the buyer of a small business. A buyer buying a business might include the following criteria: generate an annual income of $75,000; require no more than 50 hours work per week; be suitable for a husband and wife working together, etc. For a buyer who owns an existing business and wishes to expand, such criteria might include: increasing market share; increasing the number of customers; lowering fixed costs; using idle plant capacity; expanding the product line; improving production capacity; and improving distribution channels.

Once your criteria have been developed, then, based on your skills, interests, and abilities, you need to decide what kind of business to go into (manufacturing, wholesaling, retailing, or service) and focus on a specific type of business within that area. Assume that, based on your

12

knowledge of horticulture, you decide to buy a flower shop (i.e., to operate at the retail level) and to begin a search for the right shop within a certain geographic area. You might proceed by a variety of means, including cold calling, advertising, meeting with business brokers, and contacting family, friends, acquaintances, professionals, and anyone else who might have a lead.

After finding several potential flower shops to choose among, how do you evaluate them against the acquisition criteria? First, you need to get information, lots of information. For example, you need a description of the kind of business being conducted (e.g., what flower wire services are involved), the amount of sales, the number of employees, growth prospects, sales and marketing techniques, and so on. You should then rank the prospects by the criteria. If one criterion is location, how does the location of prospect 1 compare to that of prospect 3? To narrow the field down more, you'll need information in four major categories: operations, personnel, management, and finances. Since you'll have access to a good deal of proprietary information, you may be asked to sign a confidentiality statement.

Next, it's time to value the business. As is discussed in Key 22, there are a number of ways to do this. Some approaches look strictly at the assets of the business (asset-based valuations), some look strictly at the income stream generated by the business (earnings-based valuations), and some are hybrids. The value of the business is not necessarily related directly to the ultimate price paid for the business; this depends on many factors, including how desperate the seller is for cash, how long the business has been on the market, what other offers the seller has received, and whether the buyer feels he or she can make a go of an otherwise unprofitable business.

Now, it's time to negotiate. You make an offer, one that is lower than the asking price to allow room for negotiation. You should discuss terms. Will the purchase be all cash? Will there be a deposit, with the balance financed by lenders, by others, or by the seller? What interest rate will be applied, and what is the payback period? Will the seller expect a first mortgage on the assets? All of these factors affect your ability to get financing and therefore the price. For example, if you are putting a small amount down with the balance financed by the seller on reasonable terms, maybe you can afford to pay more. You should be sure you can meet the monthly payments; it's not unusual for employees, customers, and suppliers to stop dealing with a business after a change in ownership, and you may experience a sharp decline in sales. When you are negotiating with a bank for a loan, the bank will expect a detailed business plan setting forth projected sales.

An offer should clearly set forth what is being transferred and for what price and contain a warranty that the seller has a good, clear, and marketable title to the business being sold and that at the time physical possession is delivered, all equipment will be in working order and the premises will pass all inspections necessary to conduct the business. The offer should designate an escrow holder, and the escrow holder should be authorized to make any transactions necessary to finalize the sale. Other points to consider: will you assume any existing obligations of the seller? Is inventory included in the sale? How is the inventory level to be determined—by the seller and you together, by an independent service, with the cost shared equally between you, or in some other way? Who is to pay any applicable sales or use tax owed on fixtures and equipment? Usually the buyer pays the sales or use tax on fixtures and equipment at time of settlement. All other taxes and similar expenses are generally pro-rated as of the date of transfer.

The level of detail in an offer depends on whether it is just an initial offer (accompanied by a deposit to be cashed if the offer is accepted), a letter of intent, a broker-prepared offer to purchase, or something more. More often, an agreement prepared at this early stage contains only some of the details mentioned above. Your lawyer will prepare a much more detailed document later on. Clearly, the more points you agree to early on, the fewer points you will need to negotiate later. In any event, there should be an escape clause allowing you to conduct a review of the books and records and to pull back from the deal based on what is discovered. This is called the "books and records" contingency. There should also be a "financing contingency," which means that if financing cannot be obtained, the deal is off, and a "lease contingency," allowing you to withdraw the offer if a suitable lease cannot be negotiated with the landlord. The lease problem arises in the case of a sale of assets; in the case of a sale of stock, the lease should pass to the new owners without the landlord's consent, but you should double check the lease to be sure.

Other documents may be required as well. There should be a contingency removal clause to be executed once the various contingencies have been satisfied. For example, a clause may specify that the sale depends on satisfactory lease arrangements being made. Once the lease has been successfully negotiated, this contingency should be removed. You may need an addendum to the contract if, for example, the books and records review cannot be conducted in the period specified is the contract. Most states' bulk sales acts require that the business's creditors be notified. The theory is that a seller might be tempted to skip town without paying off the creditors. If this happens and you, the buyer, failed to comply with the bulk sales act, the creditors may legally go after the business's assets even after the ownership change. Telling creditors that a bulk sale is to occur is not without risk, however; the creditors may suddenly cancel credit lines or refuse to continue selling products. Thus, you need to assess whether compliance with this law should be waived; just make sure your attorney has carefully looked into this.

You will have to raise the funds to buy the business, of course, and your bank will have lots of questions about the new business, about you, and about your collateral. Even if the bank turns down your application, you can consider family members, friends, other banks, the Small Business Administration (SBA) programs, and other governmental sources, and, most important, the seller. In any case, you should avoid putting up your personal assets as collateral, putting up a personal guarantee, or having someone else cosign the debt. You of course hope the assets of the business will serve as sufficient collateral; whether this is true depends on the size of the down payment and on other factors.

Once you have made an offer, reached an agreement, and obtained financing, it is necessary to work out the final details. Even before closing takes place, you should meet with the current employees and others to prepare them for the ownership change. There is a lot to do— from obtaining a new set of licenses to getting a new phone service started. At the closing, a number of documents are executed, depending on whether the deal is an asset purchase or a stock purchase. If it's an asset deal, the detailed purchase agreement is signed, along with a bill of sale absolute. If there is seller financing, the buyer must sign a promissory note secured by the assets of the business as reflected in a security agreement and financing statement, and possibly a personal guarantee as well. If a new lease has been negotiated, it may be executed at the same time as the purchase agreement; if the buyer is incorporated, the landlord will likely require a personal guarantee from the shareholder(s). (Again, make every effort to avoid this.) In the case of an asset sale by a corporate owner, the seller's board of directors approve the deal and minutes are executed to reflect this. In the case of a stock sale, each selling shareholder decides whether to sell his or her shares, and no such approval is required. (Of course, if a minority shareholder decides not to sell out, that can mean trouble later on since the minority shareholder has certain rights, including the right to inspect the books and records.) You will issue a check made payable to the selling shareholder or shareholders in exchange for their shares; the shares are then endorsed by the seller and cancelled with new shares issued in your name. Be careful with the endorsement because the newly issued certificates will need to track it. If the new certificate is to be issued to "John

Doe and Mary Doe, joint tenants with right of survivorship," the endorsement should reflect this. If the seller in a stock sale agrees to finance some or all of the purchase price, that seller will undoubtedly demand a pledge agreement to protect his or her interest in the event of default on a payment. With the pledged shares as collateral, the selling shareholder has the option to take back the corporation as is without the need to foreclose.

After closing takes place, there are many more details to wrap up. Employees may be concerned about the possible loss of their jobs or the diminution of benefits, and you should handle such concerns directly. The acquisition process ends not with the closing but when the business and its new management are accepted in the community. The experience you acquire when buying an existing business will prove invaluable if you ever become a seller yourself.

6

THE ACQUISITION PROCESS: THE SELLER'S VIEW

First and foremost, you must decide whether you really want to sell your business. This requires that you determine that you really want to sell and that you can afford to sell. If you conclude that you are ready, willing and able to sell, you must next decide on the conditions of sale—whether stock or assets are to be sold, and, if assets, what assets are to be included, and for what price. The final determination is to whom you will sell the business. If it is a family-owned business and you wish to keep it that way, you need to work out the ownership succession. If you wish to sell to a non-family member, then you obviously must find a buyer.

Once you have decided to sell, to whom should this information be conveyed? Some owners choose not to tell their employees that a sale is being considered until late in the process; in extreme cases, employees first learn of the sale in the newspapers. One school of thought holds that letting employees know of an impending sale early on fosters a sense of job insecurity and encourages everything from indifferent job performance to mass resignations. Another school of thought argues that it is a good idea for the employees to be prepared for visits by prospective buyers as well as for the inevitable transition; in addition, a current employee may wish to buy the business and, as someone likely to ensure the company's continued success, he or she might be an ideal choice.

If you can't find a family member or an employee interested in buying your business, how do you find a buyer? Selling a business involves the same marketing skills as any other sale. Beyond word-of-mouth, including talking to your friends, fellow members of clubs and fraternal organizations, and any other contacts you might have, one of the best ways to reach potential buyers is through advertising in the business sections of local and national publications, although costs must be carefully monitored. The actual advertisement should be simple but must set forth enough detail to interest a potential buyer. The type of business should be given, along with the annual sales level, the number of years the business has operated, the location, and either a price or an indication that the price is subject to negotiation. You must also include a way for possible buyers to contact you. If confidentiality is a concern, you may wish to use an answering service. Post office boxes are another option but tend not to draw as well. The most important thing to remember is to be as specific as possible without making unnecessary disclosures or concessions; saying that sales are "high" is too vague, but giving too much detail makes it obvious who the seller is and in the case of price information may compromise your negotiating position later on.

Anyone who advertises in the business opportunities section of a newspaper can expect an interesting array of responses. Some respondents will offer to pay nothing but to run the business, while others will want just the inventory and not the business itself. If you break up the business by selling the inventory, then you wind up selling at liquidation prices, and you won't have an ongoing business to convey. Other respondents are not serious buyers but are just looking around. To avoid giving out confidential information about the business to respondents who may not be serious prospects, you should qualify the buyers and focus only on serious prospects.

If you would rather have someone else find the serious prospects for you, you might contact a business broker. Although this is discussed in detail in Key 7, a few comments here might be in order. Generally, a broker represents sellers, but sometimes a buyer hires the broker, who then conducts a mail and phone campaign. Assuming that you hire the broker you will probably be asked to sign an exclusive listing of some sort. Open listings are rarely used and suffer from a lower completion rate because of the diminished effort of brokers working on such projects.

In the listing agreement, you provide the broker with a good deal of information (e.g., monthly receipts) that you warrant to be true and correct. The agreement also specifies the duration of the contract and the disposition of any deposit or down payment given to you. (For example, if the deposit is deemed to be forfeited, you might have to split it 50-50 with the broker because brokers work on straight commission and may put a lot of time into a deal that falls through at the end.) Although the listing agreement provided by the broker may look standard, be sure to have a lawyer look it over.

Brokers find buyers in a number of ways. First, a good broker receives numerous calls and letters from potential buyers, has numerous contacts in the business community, local and beyond, and knows of individuals interested in a quality business at a reasonable price. Second, brokers may advertise your business for sale. Note though that if you list with a broker who advertises your business and attracts a buyer, the broker will sell any listed business to that buyer. In other words, the buyer will probably be shown all of the businesses that might be of interest. Once a broker finds some potential buyers, he or she will personally accompany the buyers to the business and discuss it with them. In addition, the broker may ask potential buyers to sign a form that states that the broker brought the buyer and seller together. This protects the broker's commission.

Once you find a serious buyer, either alone or with the assistance of others, you should investigate the prospect carefully. Ask for references to verify the prospect's background, financial resources, education, and business experience. To repeat, do not disclose any confidential information until this background check has been completed.

As the preliminary negotiations get underway, you will

be asked for more and more information. What if the potential buyer later uses this information against you? One solution is to have prospects sign a confidentiality statement that establishes both the proprietary nature of the information provided and the penalties for using such information wrongfully.

The confidentiality agreement may be a letter or a more formal document. It outlines the purpose of the agreement (to evaluate the business of the seller for purposes of a prospective purchase). The buyer acknowledges the receipt of financial statements and other confidential and proprietary information and agrees to keep this and the fact that the sale is being contemplated confidential, and to disclose the same only to those employed or retained to evaluate the company. The buyer agrees not to disclose this information to employees other than senior officers or to outside advisers without your prior approval and to reveal the information to no one— employee or otherwise—unless that person also agrees to execute a confidentiality agreement. The buyer agrees not to make copies of any of the materials provided and, upon the conclusion of discussions, to return all of the materials to the seller, and to destroy any notes, memoranda, or reports prepared. The buyer and anyone else who signs the confidentiality agreement must acknowledge the importance of maintaining the confidentiality of the sale as well as the materials being provided and that you may suffer irreparable damage (i.e., in lost profits, customers, etc.) if any breach occurs. Since the dollar effect of such a breach may be difficult to establish, there should be a provision for liquidated damages (i.e., if you can prove a wrongful disclosure by the buyer, the damages become fixed). Always make sure that the confidentiality agreement survives any unsuccessful negotiations for your company and that anyone you wish to include does sign.

Once the negotiations are completed and you come to an agreement on price and terms, make sure your lawyer and accountant are involved early on. If it is not to be an all-cash deal, and you plan to finance part of the purchase price, you are taking quite a risk, since the buyer may run the business into the ground. If the buyer is a corporation, you may require a personal guarantee and a first mortgage on the assets. You should also ask for a cosigner. Be careful about how you describe the assets being sold both prior to and at the time of the agreement; those descriptions may form the basis for a lawsuit later on. Beware of buyers who want to put nothing down and demand exceedingly long payback periods; if your price and terms are reasonable, another buyer should come along eventually.

7

BUSINESS BROKERS

Anyone planning to sell a business must decide whether to use the services of a business broker. Although you may be able to find a buyer by advertising or by relying on your own contacts, using a business broker may be more effective in finding the best buyer. Although business brokerage is largely an unregulated business and has attracted some unqualified and untrustworthy individuals, the right broker can provide a good deal of assistance beyond matchmaking.

Some brokers deal only in the transfer of businesses, while others operate a business brokerage as part of their real estate brokerage or other business. Most brokers are paid on a commission basis, typically, 10 percent of the selling price for a small business, but others require a minimum compensation and still others operate on a flat-fee basis. Thus, a broker specializing in the transfer of liquor licenses might charge a flat fee irrespective of the actual sales price of the license; you could expect the fee to include assistance in completing the paperwork, although each side will still need its own attorney to do the legal work. Some brokers work alone, while others routinely work on a cobrokerage basis with others.

Although using a broker may reduce your net proceeds, this is not necessarily the case. If the broker gets you a higher price for your business than you could have gotten on your own, your net proceeds may be higher. Generally, using a broker offers a number of other advantages. First, an experienced broker can help in the valuation of the business and in pulling together the information necessary to market the business. For example, if you are selling a restaurant and use a broker experienced in this field, the broker will have a good sense for what the market is like in the area and what price similar restaurants have brought.

In addition, a good business broker will save you a good deal of time and aggravation by screening out the timewasters and enabling you to concentrate on the serious prospects. Of course, a poor broker may screen out some good prospects too, so you may wish to do some screening yourself.

A good business broker will preserve your confidences. Although the word may still get out that you are selling the business, or even worse, specific data may get out about the business, the likelihood of this occurring is reduced if you use a broker. A broker's reputation depends in large part on maintaining such confidences. In a typical offering circular, the business broker describes only the business, its location, financial information such as sales and profits, the asking price, financing availability, and similar matters. However, your name and address will not be divulged.

A good broker will provide a continuing stream of potential buyers and will have a list of those currently in the market for this kind of business after all, the broker makes money only if a sale goes through and therefore relies on an accurate list of serious prospects. Conversely, a good broker constantly receives requests from sellers to handle their transfers. If the business is not sold relatively quickly, the broker might lose interest and move on to more promising projects. What should happen, of course, is that the broker should level with the client, and explain why the business is not selling and what the broker intends to do to change the situation.

Conversations between a seller and a potential buyer can get bogged down over ego, over trivia, and over other concerns. The broker can transmit offers without taking them personally and can provide realistic, accurate, and timely information to both sides. Unfortunately, a poor, hungry broker can have a hidden agenda and, to see the deal go through, can actively mislead a seller or buyer.

To avoid this, buyers and sellers should always verify

the information provided to them, no matter what the broker says has been done.

Since the quality of the broker's work is dependent on the quality of the information received, the seller and the buyer should both be sure to level with the broker. As a seller, you are wasting your time and the broker's if you exaggerate sales or any other item. Similarly, as a buyer you are wasting your time and the broker's if you are not emotionally and financially ready to buy a business.

How do you choose a broker? You should feel free to inquire about the broker's qualifications and experience, length of time in the brokerage field generally and in this community in particular, expertise in this type of business, and ideas for marketing your business.

Be sure to find out what level of service the broker will provide. Will the broker help the buyer obtain financing, for example? What is included in the fee? Determine how hard the broker will try to market the business. Will it be a solo venture or a team effort, with other persons and offices joining in the task?

Try to have the actual brokerage agreement reviewed by your attorney before you sign it. The broker will probably want an exclusive right to sell, meaning that the broker gets a commission even if you find the buyer yourself. You should try to negotiate an open listing, which gives you the right to sell the business on your own or through other brokers. In such cases, the commission is due only if the broker secures the buyer. Very few brokers will agree to these terms, however. A possible intermediate solution is the exclusive agency, which prohibits you from listing with other brokers but allows you to sell directly. In any kind of exclusive agreement, though, be sure to set a time limit on the contract. The agreement can always be renewed, but if the broker is not performing properly, you need an escape clause. Further, even if the broker does not budge on the required commission level, be sure to clarify what the percentage is to be based on—the gross sales price, the net proceeds to the seller, or some other figure.

8

SHOULD THE
SELLER STAY ON?

One of the best ways to learn about an existing business is to have the former owner stay on in a consulting capacity for three to six months after you take ownership. Unless the seller literally plans to leave town or is in poor health, he or she may be willing to stay on for a limited period to help you effect a successful transition.

Having the former owner serve as a consultant can be an excellent idea, since the seller clearly knows more about the business than you do. An owner who will be staying on for a while is more likely to be forthright about the minuses associated with the business and, if and when problems do arise, may be able to offer invaluable advice. It is important, however, to set forth exactly what you expect from the seller in an employment agreement, a consulting agreement or within the purchase agreement itself.

There are various ways to compensate the seller for these services. Some favor pegging compensation to company performance, while others favor a flat fee or salary. Of course, if the former seller agrees to help with the understanding that such consultation is included in the purchase price, this should not be ruled out either.

Remember, though, that the presence of the seller can create an identity crisis for the business. All customers, suppliers, employees, and others should understand that you are making the decisions and any complaints, suggestions, or problems should be brought to your attention, not the former owner's.

9

QUALIFYING THE BUSINESS

After you decide on the kind of business you'd like to buy, you should evaluate carefully the business you are considering to determine the proper price and terms. This is not an easy task, but it's well worth the effort when it comes to avoiding subsequent problems and making sure that you'll be able to achieve a reasonable return on your investment. Evaluating a business requires four basic steps: studying the background of the seller; studying the business; examining the assets and liabilities; and examining the financial statements, licenses, and other documents.

The first question you should ask is why the seller is selling the business. Some common reasons include:

- Owner's ill health
- Owner's desire to retire or to relocate
- The changing nature of the business or the neighborhood
- Owner's desire to move on to a different business opportunity
- New competition that is squeezing out the current business
- Loss of important contracts or customers
- Recent changes in zoning or other laws

The seller may tell you that he or she is selling out because of advanced age, but the real reason may be something more ominous. For example, without signing a noncompete agreement, a key employee may have just left and may be taking a lot of customers. The effect of this may take a little time to be felt. It is up to you as the buyer, in conjunction with your advisers, to investigate the seller as soon as possible; a bad situation can

27

sometimes be turned around, but you need to know why it's a bad situation.

There is a lot you need to know about the background of the business. For example, when was the business started, who has owned the business, and how long has the current owner operated it? Ownership is one thing; management is quite another. Be sure to check out the qualifications of the various employees, any employment agreements in place, and whether the employees appear satisfied with the company.

Next, you should look at the goods or services offered by the seller. What kinds are being offered, are they popular, and what new ones are being considered? How has the market for the goods or services changed, and how has the location affected sales?

You should look at the current and future competition and consider whether the goods or services of competitors compare favorably with those of the business you are considering.

You should look at staffing patterns and whether cost savings might be achieved by cutting staff. The compensation levels should be studied and, if the company has a union, the present contract, including its expiration date, and items up for negotiation should be considered. Clearly, you need to evaluate the level of employee turnover and staff morale.

When you are qualifying a business it is important to examine each category of assets of the business: their title, value, and condition. Some of the more important assets and liabilities will be considered here.

First consider *cash and marketable securities,* although neither is generally included in the sales price. Determine whether any cash that is included is held as a compensating balance required for a loan or is freely available for use. Determine how diversified the portfolio of marketable securities is and whether any of the securities have been pledged on a loan or other agreement.

Age the *accounts receivables* by the amount of time outstanding (30 days, 60 days, 90 days) and consider the creditworthiness of the customers and their prior payment experience. If the accounts prove difficult to collect and must be turned over to a collections agency, their value will be significantly reduced. A potential buyer should also determine if any of the receivables have been factored or pledged.

Next, consider the historical and replacement cost, age and method of valuation used for inventories. Determine how the inventory is broken down between raw materials, work in progress, and finished goods and whether the inventory contains any obsolete or damaged items. Also, consider whether inventory levels can be reduced through improved management.

Next, consider *fixed assets* such as the building, machinery, and equipment, and whether such assets are owned or leased. Analyze the age of the assets, their historical and replacement cost, and what replacements appear likely in the near future.

Next, consider the *prepaid expenses* such as insurance contracts. Examine the contracts to determine if they can be assumed.

Next, consider the *customer and supplier lists.* You should ensure that you have access to all of the seller's lists, and try to meet with the principal customers and suppliers before the closing, if not before signing the contract.

The same process should be employed when considering the rest of the seller's assets, tangible and intangible. After evaluating the assets, move on to the liabilities. For *accounts payable,* determine the ages and due dates, whether available discounts have been taken, whether any liabilities are in dispute, whether any payments are in collection, and what efforts are being taken to resolve such disputes. For the *notes payable,* determine if the notes are current, if they are secured or unsecured, their terms and conditions, and whether the sale of the business will trigger an acceleration of the note.

After examining the payment schedules of *long-term liabilities,* and seeing whether any of the obligations are in default, determine if the sale will trigger acceleration of the debt. Be sure to assess the overall credit standing and rating of the seller.

The next step in qualifying a business is to obtain *financial statements* and other documentation. Thus, for example, you should have the financial statements for the past three years, if the seller has been in business that long, federal and state tax returns, and other accounting materials, such as copies of inventories taken, budgets, cash flow statements, bank statements, checkbooks, cash receipts and disbursement journals, the chart of accounts, ledgers, and journals.

Although the purpose of this inquiry is to qualify the business as a prospect and to determine whether the business warrants further analysis, as a practical matter, much of this requested material will not be available until an agreement is signed. The fundamental problem is that to determine the value of a business and whether it should be bought at all, requires a good deal of information. You may make a poor offer because of what you do not know. If the data can't be obtained prior to signing, it is important to build contingencies into the contract that enable you to back out or renegotiate based on what you discover later on.

Assuming some financial information has been obtained, how do you analyze it? First, consider the income statement and the statement of financial position or balance sheet. You should examine each category of income, such as sales, and determine if it is increasing, decreasing, or staying static. Determine if sales are cyclical or steady, whether sales are being made to a broad range of customers or are dependent on just a few, and what the company's policy is regarding sales returns and allowances. You should examine how the expenses are allocated among production, general, and administrative costs, and what expenses can be reduced or eliminated with improved management.

There are many methods of analysis for examining an income statement. For example, you can compare the current financial data to historical data for the company, or for the industry as a whole. Such methods are also useful in examining the balance sheet. One such tool, the analysis of various financial ratios, is considered here.

- **Liquidity ratios.** Liquidity refers to the ability to convert an asset to cash readily without losing the principal invested in it. The classic liquidity ratio is the current ratio, current assets/current liabilities. The problem with this ratio is that some current assets aren't that liquid, so the quick ratio—quick assets (cash + accounts receivable) divided by the current liabilities may be a better indicator. The most liquid asset, cash, divided by current liabilities, gives you the cash ratio. It is generally a good idea to determine the percentage composition of the current assets, broken down, for example, among cash, accounts receivable, inventory, and prepaid assets.
- **Leverage ratios.** Leverage refers to the use of borrowed funds to magnify a gain or loss on the principal amount invested. Two commonly used ratios for evaluating leverage are the funded debt ratio and the debt/equity ratio. The funded debt ratio is computed by dividing long-term debt by a prospect's tangible net worth (total equity minus the intangibles). The debt/equity ratio is computed by dividing total debt by the net worth. The IRS looks to this ratio to determine if a corporation is thinly capitalized, and so should potential buyers.
- **Profitability ratios.** Profitability refers simply to the profits thrown off by the business. First, determine the gross profit (sales minus the cost of goods sold). Dividing the gross profit by sales results in the gross profit margin. Dividing operating profit from the income statement by sales results in the operating profit margin. You can assess profitability by dividing net income by sales, by total capitalization, or by assets. Another common profitability ratio is the return on equity, which is found by dividing net income minus preferred dividends, if any, by the common shareholders' equity.
- **Activity ratios.** Activity ratios are useful for determining how many times a particular item turns over in a period. For example, to compute the average collection

period, multiply the accounts receivable by 365 and divide the result by the annual credit sales. If the answer is 45 days and the standard terms in the industry call for payment within 30 days, such a figure may indicate a real problem. Similarly, to compute the days that purchases made by a prospect are outstanding, multiply the accounts payable by 365 and divide the result by the annual purchases. Again, the result, expressed in days, should be compared to the historical record of the seller and to the industry norm.

- **Inventory ratios.** The inventory turnover ratio is generally computed by dividing cost of goods sold by the average ending inventory. Asset turnover is computed by dividing sales by the average assets. If you multiply the asset turnover ratio by the operating profit margin discussed earlier, the result—"earning power"—measures the prospect's earning power on the assets.

Now that you have evaluated the owner of the business and the business itself, along with the assets and liabilities and financials, you should consider the relevant licenses and other documents. Of particular importance here is what licenses are required to operate the business and whether they may be assumed. For example, liquor licenses may be bought and sold, although you must complete extensive applications, pay a fee, and pass a background check. Similarly, look at the certificate of occupancy and occupational licenses.

Assuming that you have qualified a business as warranting a further look, the business analysis is next. Many checklists have been developed to aid in this process, and the specific items included hinge on the industry involved. Generally, a functional breakdown is best (e.g., sales/ marketing, management, personnel, operations, and financial/accounting), although you should work with your advisers to develop a checklist most relevant to the kind of business being analyzed.

Let's take as an example the possible purchase of a restaurant. Assume you have analyzed the market and have narrowed the choices down to buying a fast-food place, a carryout restaurant, or a breakfast place. You have decided to limit your choices to breakfast places and you need a basis for comparing such restaurants.

- Beginning with the sales/marketing function, you might examine daily sales reports to track how sales have improved over time and what items on the menu seem to be the best sellers. If sales are poor, you might turn to market research in the area to evaluate the need for such a restaurant in the area. Perhaps the restaurant has a poor reputation for service or has been poorly advertised, in which case the advertising budget needs to be increased.
- Moving on to management, you might consider whether the present management has made optimum use of the facilities and personnel. Perhaps the restaurant needs to be open more days for more hours requiring additional help. Does the present management command the respect of the employees? Does the present owner comply with federal, state, and local laws and regulations (e.g., health codes)?
- To evaluate personnel, determine what the turnover is for the waiters/cooks, dishwashers, janitors, and others. How loyal will they be in the event of a change in ownership? Try to determine how motivated they are to serve the public and how well trained they appear to be. Is there a company handbook in place explaining the rules? Indifferent service or employees who don't show up on time—so that the restaurant can't open on time—can quickly antagonize potential customers.
- Evaluate the restaurant's operations. Consider its quality control practices and whether the customers appear satisfied. Customer evaluations can be helpful in this regard. Consider whether the seller is adequately insured and what the claims experience has been (e.g., for products liability). In a different aspect of operations, who are the restaurant's suppliers? Are competitive bids being solicited for food products?
- In reviewing accounting and financial issues, look at what internal controls are in place. Are standard recipes and portions used? Are prenumbered checks used by the servers to record all sales? Are all used checks

surrendered to the cashier, and is there an independent comparison of cash and the servers' checks with the record of sales? Is a receiving clerk employed to verify that merchandise received matches what is shown on the receiving memo? Are tips being reported according to federal tax law? (Employees must report tips of $20 or more to an employer; the employer in turn must include employees' reported tips for social security and employment tax purposes on the quarterly tax returns and is liable for the employer's portion of FICA tax).

The idea then is for you to know as much about the business as possible in order to know what questions to ask. Break up the questions into subject areas, and make sure the questions are answered before committing to a purchase. Take careful notes, as they form the basis for representations and warranties concerning the condition of the company now and, as far as is known, in the future (See Key 42). If the seller appears to be reluctant to disclose information, be careful.

10

LOCATION AND LEASE ANALYSIS

The value of any small business depends to a large extent on its location. There are two major aspects of location analysis: market/neighborhood analysis and building analysis.

Beginning with the market/neighborhood evaluation, you should look at the demographics of the community as a whole and of the immediate area of the business in particular. Consider your customers. How will they get to your place of business and is the location accessible to them? If you will be wholesaling some products, you will need a location that is convenient for your major customers and that large trucks can easily reach from the major highways. Do you expect your customers to come to you from the immediate area (as is the case with a grocery store), or will they be coming from greater distances (as is the case with a store specializing in expensive antiques)? Will your business fit in the neighborhood? (A toy store probably wouldn't fit in well in a retirement village.) If the business is located downtown, does the town close down after dark? Spend plenty of time in the proposed location, not just in the daytime but in the evenings when you expect to be open, and evaluate traffic patterns.

What about safety? Will the neighborhood attract customers or tend to scare them off? Are competitors fleeing to greener, or at least safer, pastures? What is the school system like? Many large corporations are relocating to cities with better educational systems, not only because the potential workers in the area are better educated but because the company can offer the employees a superior school system as a form of fringe benefit.

What are the building and immediate neighborhood like? A newsstand can be a gold mine in a busy office building but a money-loser if the building is barely occupied. Such a tenant may want to postpone finalizing the lease until the occupancy level of the building is known. Similarly, a coin-operated laundry might do well in a neighborhood where few residents own washers and dryers; however, if it's hard to find a parking space or if it's necessary to keep putting quarters in a meter, your potential customers may not think it's worth the hassle and may find a different laundromat.

After you've evaluated the potential market for your product or service and have found a fine location, consider the building itself. Is the facility properly zoned for what you need to do? Are the facilities adequate for shipping and receiving? Are there any problems with the structure itself? Is there sufficient space for your sign so that drivers-by will be able to find your business? What about air-conditioning—in some office buildings, if the prime tenant or owner doesn't do business on the weekends, it's assumed that no one else will either, and other tenants who want the air conditioning turned on must provide advance notice. Who will be the tenants next to and below you? Are they noisy? How thick are the walls? If you will be situated within a mall, who are the major tenants and what kinds of leases do they have? Is there adequate storage space? Develop your own list of questions based on your business's needs.

Assuming that the market/neighborhood evaluation and the physical set up all appear to check out, what about the lease you are about to negotiate? Much depends on what you've already found out. You may well be concerned if the lease allows competing or otherwise inappropriate business to operate in the same building. For example a check-cashing store may not fit in well next to a high-priced boutique. As you check out the neighborhood and the building, you should talk with your future neighbors about other businesses that have occupied the building, typical rents in the building and in the area, the period remaining on the seller's lease, etc.

Before signing anything, you should have your attorney check out the landlord, including the existence of any prior mortgages. This is especially true if you are going to be the prime tenant. If you're buying the shares of stock of an existing business, the lease should go with the transfer of stock. If the lease has been personally guaranteed by the seller, the seller will want to be released from this guarantee. If you're buying assets, the purchase agreement should contain an escape clause known as a lease contingency, that says that your contractual obligations are subject to your being able to assume the lease or to negotiate a new one without a personal guarantee. Generally, this means that you'll meet with the landlord to determine whether the terms of the existing or renegotiated lease are satisfactory. If such a lease can't be negotiated, the sales contract may be voided and all deposits returned, releasing the parties from any further obligations to each other.

As a practical matter, although leases are generally nonassignable without prior landlord consent, many leases do stipulate that such consent is not to be unreasonably withheld. If you do have to renegotiate a lease. make sure you've checked out comparable rents in the area (rents may have come down), and make sure the rental commitment is consistent with industry norms and your expected profit margin. (e.g., some businesses can withstand a higher rent per square foot than others.) Incidentally, rent quoted at, for example, $8 per square foot, means that if you lease 1000 square feet, the annual rent will be $8000. Obviously, you'll need to find out what's included in the $8000. For example, in a gross lease of $1000 per month, that's what you pay per month, plus applicable sales tax. However, there are other forms of commercial leases, such as a triple net lease, in which you as a tenant are responsible for an allocated share of certain common expenses. A knowledgeable real estate broker specializing in commercial properties can be of great assistance to you in interpreting the precise terms of your lease.

11

CHOICE OF ENTITY

This key introduces you to the considerations involved in selecting the legal structure through which you will do business. Broadly speaking, there are three forms in use in the United States today—the sole proprietorship, the partnership, and the corporation.

A sole proprietorship is a business owned by an individual, either in his or her own name or in a trade name. The income of the business is the individual proprietor's income, and any loss of the business is the individual owner's loss. Profits from the business are taxed as income to the individual on his or her own individual tax return and are reported on Schedule C of Form 1040. Losses from the business are deductible against an individual's income. A proprietor operating under a trade name, trademark, or service mark is required to register the name or mark by filing a notice with the state and, if operating in interstate commerce, possibly with the U.S. Patent and Trademark Office in Washington, D.C.

The principal advantages of the sole proprietorship are ease of formation and operation. There is no additional recordkeeping involved, since a proprietorship is not a separate entity, and there are fewer tax requirements than apply to a partnership or corporation. The principal disadvantages of the proprietorship form are that the proprietor has unrestricted and unlimited liability for obligations arising out of the operation of the business and that the enterprise ends upon the death of the owner. A surviving spouse, for example, may inherit all of the assets of the business but must start a new business, which means obtaining new licenses and tax numbers and beginning credit from scratch in order to continue the business.

A partnership is a joint participation by more than one individual in a business. A partnership may be formed either informally by oral agreement or formally by written agreement, although the latter is clearly advised. The partnership is not taxed separately from the individuals who comprise the firm but is required to file an informational return, Form 1065, due on or before the 15th day of the fourth month following the close of the tax year of the business (for a calender-year business, April 15).

Each of the partners has unlimited personal liability for the obligations, claims, torts, and liabilities of the firm. Further, if one partner dies, the partnership may be forced out of business; the surviving heirs can force the sale of their share of the assets of the firm even if the surviving partner needs them to carry on the business. If the surviving partner does not have the funds to buy the heirs out, the business may have to be dissolved. (With a corporation, the heirs inherit only stock; with properly executed buy-sell documents, the business can continue.) In the case of a limited partnership, in addition to at least one general partner who is liable for the debts of the partnership, there are limited partners whose liability is limited to their investment in the partnership. A limited partnership may not be created by a mere agreement between the partners; a certificate of registration must be filed with the secretary of state's office in the state in which it is to operate.

The corporation differs from a sole proprietorship and a partnership primarily in that it is regarded by law as having an existence separate and distinct from its members or shareholders and thus is responsible for its own debts. This means that the corporation's shareholders are not personally responsible for the corporation's debts; the shareholders' liability is limited to their investment in the corporation. Also, because it is a separate entity, the corporation continues despite the death or incapacity of its shareholders or the transfer of their shares; that is, the corporation is capable of continuing perpetually. The management and control of the corporation's affairs are centralized in a board of directors and officers who act under the board's authority. Although the shareholders generally elect the board members, they cannot directly control the board's activities, except in a closely-held corporation (one with few stockholders) where state law permits such direct management. Finally, shareholders of a corporation can freely transfer their shares, although, as a practical matter, the market for shares in a closely-held corporation may be fairly limited and the existence of buy-sell agreements may limit the transferability of shares. A corporation, and all of its assets, can be transferred by a simple assignment of a stock certificate, while all of the assets of a proprietorship or partnership must be individually transferred.

If a corporation does not make a special election, it is taxed as a regular (C) corporation, resulting in taxation at the corporate level and, when dividends are paid, at the shareholder level. This double taxation can be minimized by paying wages and other benefits to employee-shareholders. In addition, if the corporation is eligible, it can choose S corporation status, in which it retains its corporate advantage of limited liability while avoiding corporate-level taxation since the income or losses of the company are taxed to the owners individually, according to their respective shareholdings.

Other disadvantages associated with the corporate form, in addition to the double taxation imposed by the corporate tax, are the expense associated with formation, the complexity of operation, and the difficulties associated with corporate dissolution. A corporation is required to file its own tax return; owners must be careful to keep their personal finances separate from those of the corporate business. There are extra expenses for operating in the corporate form, such as the fee paid when filing the annual report; and a variety of procedural hurdles must be met to voluntarily dissolve the business. It is possible to deliberately have the corporation be "involuntarily dissolved" by not filing the annual report, but care must be exercised. Even corporations that have never begun business may find themselves liable for filing tax returns or other documents, and the failure to do so may result in penalties. Certain aspects can be either an advantage or a disadvantage, depending on the circumstances. Thus, a corporation has its own credit rating which can be better or worse than that of the owners. A corporation can file bankruptcy without harming the owner's credit; conversely, an owner's credit may be bad but without affecting the corporation's good credit rating.

12

OVERVIEW OF BUY-SELL AGREEMENTS

Before an agreement can be reached between buyer and seller, both must agree on the method of transfer. The sale of an unincorporated business is ordinarily accomplished through a transfer of assets, while a sale of an incorporated business can be accomplished through a transfer of either assets or stock. This key discusses the principal factors influencing the means of transfer for a corporation.

In a transfer of assets, the seller passes title to particular assets; thus, in addition to the buy-sell agreement, there is also a bill of sale. An individual purchaser will generally incorporate before entering into the agreement in order to have all of the assets in the corporate name. If, because of time constraints, you have to buy a business in your own name rather than in the name of the corporation, the contract can be assigned to the newly-formed corporation after the transfer. If, however, you operate the business as a proprietorship and later decide to incorporate, this incorporation is considered an incorporation of an existing business and all of the bulk sale and other requirements must be met again; further, every document, from stationery to insurance contracts, will need to be modified. You are thus well advised to choose the form of organization early on and stick with it.

In a transfer of corporate stock, the ownership transfer is effected by endorsing the existing shares of stock and issuing new shares in the new shareholder's name. New directors and officers are then elected to run the business, and a new registered agent and office are specified. Instead of having to retitle the business one asset or group

43

of assets at a time, all that ordinarily has to be retitled in a stock transfer is the shares themselves.

A number of factors influence the choice of transfer method. Some of the most important are:

- **Subject of the transfer.** If, for example, only a portion of the business is to be conveyed, it makes more sense to convey assets, leaving the corporation in place with whatever assets remain. However, in the case of an asset sale, instruments of transfer are needed for each asset or group of assets, detailed schedules of assets may have to be prepared, and, if numerous parcels of real estate are involved, the cost of title insurance and title reports may be huge.

- **Financing.** If the corporation is highly leveraged and its assets have been pledged to secure the loan, the secured party's approval may be necessary to sell the assets. In fact, as a condition of transfer, the lender may be able to demand payment, or at least renegotiation of the terms of the loan. In such case, a sale of stock is preferable.

- **Leases.** If assets are being sold, the buyer usually has to negotiate a new lease with the landlord. In a stock sale, however, landlord approval is generally not required. Assuming that the unexpired portion of the lease is significant and that the lease terms are favorable, a sale of stock may be indicated.

- **Contracts.** The corporation may have signed certain contracts that, like the lease, may not be assigned without the approval of the other contracting party; in fact, some agreements may expressly prohibit transfer. For example, a distributorship agreement may say, "Neither this Agreement, nor the rights herein conferred on the Distributor, may be transferred or assigned to others." Again, a sale of stock may be indicated.

- **Employee benefit plans.** Employee benefit plans are generally employer-sponsored plans that provide benefits if an employee should die, become disabled or sick, or retire. Such plans play an important role in the employee's total compensation. If the selling corporation has a decent program in place, perhaps one even better than the purchaser's, it may be worthwhile for you to buy stock rather than assets and to keep the existing plan in place within the framework of a corporate subsidiary. Conversely, under the federal Multiemployer Plan Withdrawal Liability Act, a seller may have continuing liability under a multiemployer retirement plan even after disposing of the assets of the business. This liability can be avoided if certain requirements regarding continuing contributions by the buyer are met.

- **Exposure.** For the most part, you as a purchaser of assets know what you are buying, and you hope that hidden liabilities will not be bought along with the liabilities. To minimize your risk of exposure, you should consider incorporation, which insulates your personal assets from the liabilities, disclosed and undisclosed, of the acquired business. Although some protection is provided for buyers in nonfraudulent arm's-length transactions that satisfy the applicable bulk sales act (see Key 21), satisfying the requirements of that law does not eliminate the need to do a complete search of the records. Your attorney should verify that the seller is able to convey and has title to the particular assets. Your attorney should also make sure that clauses in the contract protect you against this and part of the purchase price should be held in escrow and not paid over at the time of closing. Although in general, if you want to minimize the risk of subsequent exposure, an asset purchase is thus advised, certain kinds of claims, such as for products liability, may even apply in an asset transfer. Under the so-called product line rule, a purchaser of all or substantially all of the assets of another corporation is liable for defects in products manufactured and distributed by the seller if (a) following the sale, the seller is converted into a shell (an inactive corporation); (b) the purchaser holds itself out to the public as a successor to the original company by manufacturing the same product under a similar name; and (c) the purchaser benefits from the goodwill of the seller following the transaction.

- **Charters and licenses.** You may wish to effect a stock transfer if the corporation holds a valuable charter or license or if it has a good credit rating. If you buy a business with a favorable experience rating for unemployment compensation tax purposes, it may be possible to carry forward that rate. If approvals need to be obtained from a state agency or other regulator, this may affect the form of the sale as well; in any case, the seller is expected to cooperate in signing any papers necessary for you to obtain the approval.
- **Necessary consents.** If all of the shares are owned by one person, conveying stock is a simple process; if there are many shareholders, it may be difficult to get all to agree to sell their shares. Although buying less than 100 percent ownership in a small corporation is not unheard of, allowing minority shareholders to remain after you take control can cause real problems, particularly because of their statutory right to inspect the corporation's books. If the minority shareholders do not agree to sell out their interests, you may be better off buying assets instead of stock.
- **Regulatory issues.** Regulatory statutes may or may not affect the transfer decision. For example, the antitrust laws apply to acquisitions involving not only corporations but proprietorships and partnerships as well. Section 7A of the federal Clayton Act requires notification of the Federal Trade Commission and the Justice Department in advance of the acquisition and require you to observe a waiting period before completing a nonexempt merger or acquisition (i.e., one that is subject to antitrust laws). Although the "size of person" and "size of acquisition" tests in the law may make this statute inapplicable to a small acquisition, given the severe penalties associated with an antitrust violation, any proposed acquisition with antitrust consequences should be reviewed by an expert in the field.
- **Tax aspects.** From the buyer's standpoint, it is generally preferable to purchase assets instead of stock, because goodwill and going concern intangible assets simply wait on the firm's balance sheet until the business is

sold, providing no immediate tax benefit to the buyer. Thanks to the Tax Reform Act of 1986 it is generally irrelevant to a seller whether assets or stock is sold, since there is no distinction made between capital gains and other income. It can make a big difference to the buyer, however.

- **Other aspects.** You as the buyer have the responsibility for ensuring that there are no unpleasant surprises down the road that could have been avoided by greater thoroughness before consummating the deal, and this is true regardless of the form of the transfer. For example, in the travel agency business, you have to be careful that an employee has not "stolen from the business" by selling a ticket, and then voiding out the rest of the copies, and claiming the ticket was never sold. If the employee does a cash sale, and keeps the funds, it may be awhile, before the agency finds out, and the employee gets caught. The agency meanwhile will be on the hook for the ticket which is used by the customer. If the business is sold, the buyer may find himself liable to the airlines for the supposedly "voided" tickets. The answer lies in being careful in one's review of the business (one should always ask to see all copies of supposedly voided tickets) and careful in negotiating the contract to clarify who will be responsible in such circumstances.

13

STOCK PURCHASE: LEGAL REVIEW (Part I)

Early in the process of deciding whether to purchase the stock of a small business, you should ask to inspect physically the stock certificate(s) that the seller claims to own. Moreover, the seller should state in the letter of intent that the company is a duly and validly existing corporation under the laws of the particular state, that the seller has good and marketable title to the shares with full right and authority to sell and transfer the shares, that the shares are free from any pledge, lien, or encumbrance, and are not subject to any adverse claim, that the seller's shares represent all of the issued and outstanding stock of the business (assuming this is the intent of the deal), that no outstanding subscriptions exist, and that there are no outstanding assignments or rights, proxies, or any other form of stock power issued and arising from the seller's shares. Later, these representations or warranties will be formalized in a stock purchase agreement.

In getting ready for the closing, your attorney needs to check things out by reviewing all corporate documents, such as the articles, bylaws, minutes, and record book. Some of the documents, such as the share certificates themselves, refer to still other documents, such as share transfer agreements.

Initially, your attorney should examine the articles of incorporation of the selling corporation. A corporation organized in one state is said to be a domestic corporation in that state and a foreign corporation in all others; a foreign corporation wishing to do business in other states must apply for permission to do so. The corporation must be actually transacting ordinary corporate business to be subject to such restrictions. Thus, merely holding real property within a state or selling property by mail order does not generally require such approval. If it turns out that a certificate of authority should have been obtained, the corporation's legal rights may be limited (for example, it may not be able to bring a lawsuit) until it obtains the certificate. Thus, your attorney must check that all certificates of authority have been obtained and are not delinquent in any manner.

The attorney should have a true and correct copy of the articles of incorporation, as well as a receipt showing that they have been duly filed with the department of state's office. The articles, unlike the bylaws, are a matter of public record, and the department of state's office keeps a record of any changes to the articles, including any name changes. The articles themselves cover a number of points, such as the name (generally, a word evidencing corporateness, such as "corp." must be included); duration (generally, corporations have perpetual existence from the date the articles are filed although some corporations have only a fixed duration and others have a delayed effective date); purpose (generally, corporations are organized "for the purpose of transacting any or all lawful business," although some corporations, such as professional service corporations, have more limited purposes); capital stock (generally, in the articles, all that is indicated is the number of authorized shares and whether the shares are par or no-par, although some corporations have more than one class or series of shares); preemptive rights (authorizing each shareholder, subject to state law, to purchase a pro rata share at the price offered to others to prevent dilution of the shareholder's interest in the corporation); and other sections dealing with the initial registered agent and office (important for determining who shall be served legal papers), the initial board of directors and incorporators, how the articles may be amended, and various other specialized provisions.

Next, your attorney should carefully consider the corporate bylaws that detail the continuing regulatory structure of the business and the management of its affairs. Typically, the bylaws cover such points as the location of the principal offices, meetings of the board of directors and the shareholders, certificates for shares, the corporate seal, dividends, the corporate fiscal year, and amendments to the bylaws.

The attorney should be on the lookout for any potential conflicts between the corporate bylaws and articles and for any special quorum or voting requirements. Corporations with more than one owner often require more than a simple quorum and so that an action requiring $\frac{2}{3}$ approval would effectively give a 40 percent owner veto power. Most buyers of small businesses buy all of the outstanding stock, but if a minority interest will remain after closing, analyzing such restrictions is crucial.

Next, the attorney examines the minutes of the various meetings. Supposedly, the organizational meeting will have been held, the bylaws and seal adopted and the officers and directors elected, the S election authorization made if applicable, a bank account approved, and other such matters accomplished. The attorney will verify whether these crucial meetings were actually held and the other actions carried out. Some corporations pass a corporate resolution approving S corporation status, but don't bother to send in the Form 2553 to the IRS—a major mistake.

Assuming that the organizational steps were carried out, the attorney will move on to the annual meetings of the directors and shareholders and determine if proper notice was given, if the meetings were actually held, and if minutes were maintained. For example, any shareholder loans and any amendments to the bylaws should have been properly recorded.

Similarly, minutes of any special meetings of the directors and shareholders are examined to determine for what purpose they were held, if proper notice was given, and if the minutes were properly maintained.

14

STOCK PURCHASE: LEGAL REVIEW (Part II)

After reviewing all documents concerning incorporation and annual meetings, your attorney should carefully review the stock seal (individualized for the corporation), the stock certificates, and the stock transfer ledger. A seal is generally circular and contains the corporate name, the state, and the year of incorporation. Although a seal is no longer legally required in many states as a means of formalizing a particular document, banks and others still require a corporate seal, so most corporations should have one in usable condition.

The stock certificates give evidence of an ownership interest and are important for determining who can vote, receive dividends, and participate in other shareholder functions, such as voting on amendments, approving the sale, exchange, lease, or other disposition of substantially all assets and authorizing mergers or consolidations.

Generally, there are two types of securities: debt securities, which create a debtor-creditor relationship, and equity securities, which create an ownership relationship. There are three basic types of debt securities: debentures (long-term unsecured debt securities which have indentures to protect the rights of the debenture holders); bonds (long-term secured securities, generally secured by some sort of collateral, such as real property); and notes, which offer a shorter term than either debentures or bonds. Like long-term securities, notes may either be secured or unsecured.

There are two types of equity securities: common stock which usually carries with it the right to vote and to receive dividends; and preferred stock, which entitles the holder to a fixed annual dividend before any dividend is paid to the holders of the common stock and to preferences with respect to assets or dividends over other classes of shares.

Shares of stock may be authorized, issued, or outstanding. Authorized shares are those shares that a corporation is permitted to issue pursuant to its articles; a corporation may not issue more shares than are actually authorized. Issued shares are those shares that have been sold to shareholders; outstanding shares are those currently held by shareholders. If a corporation purchases (or redeems) its own shares, it either cancels those shares, restores them to unissued status, or places them in the corporate treasury.

Repurchased shares, cancelled by the corporation, are said not to exist and may not be reissued. If the corporation restores the shares to unissued status, the shares are considered authorized and may later be reissued. If the corporation neither cancels the shares nor restores them to unissued status, the shares are considered treasury shares (i.e., authorized and issued but not outstanding). Such shares may subsequently be sold although their holders may not vote nor receive dividends.

15

STOCK PURCHASE: LEGAL REVIEW (Part III)

Consideration and par value are two important concepts for you as a prospective buyer to understand. The consideration is the initial payment made for the shares by subscribers, or initial investors, when the corporation is being organized. Prior to incorporation, people may agree to purchase a specified number of shares of stock at a certain price, called the subscription price. Since an unpaid subscription price is considered a debt to the corporation, your attorney should verify that each subscription has been fully satisfied.

When the corporation is formed, the board of directors is empowered to issue shares on the corporation's behalf for the consideration and price it deems fair. Subject to state law, only certain types of consideration are eligible. In many states shares may be issued only for money, property, and labor actually performed; thus promissory notes and promises of future services are not acceptable. Other states do permit shares to be issued for notes or future services, however. The board has the authority to value the consideration received; at the organizational meeting, both the number of shares issued and the consideration paid for them is indicated. As regards the quantity of consideration necessary, the concepts of par value and no-par value become relevant.

Par value is an arbitrary amount assigned to the shares by the articles of incorporation. It may be any amount and may or may not reflect the fair market value of the shares; rather, it reflects the minimum amount of consideration for which the shares may be issued and is designed to be a cushion for the benefit of the creditors. Stock sold for less that its par value is said to be watered, and the shareholder is liable for the difference, although, as a practical matter, in small corporations the stockholders will have fully paid in at least the par value. If shares are issued for more than their par value, the excess goes to a capital surplus account. For example if a corporation issues 1,000 shares of stock with a par value of $1 in exchange for $10,000, $1,000 goes into the stated capital account and $9,000 goes into the capital surplus account. (The distinction is important; corporate stated capital may not be used to pay dividends.)

Certain shares, known as no-par shares, do not have a par value. The board of directors is permitted to issue them for whatever consideration that it, in its reasonable, good-faith judgment, deems appropriate. There is no floor below which the price may not be set. Further, the board may allocate a portion of the consideration to the capital surplus account.

In summary, the consideration for shares with a par value is whatever amount at or above the par value is fixed by the board while the consideration for no-par shares is whatever is fixed by the board. In either case, the judgment of the board as to the value of the consideration received for the shares is conclusive in the absence of fraud in the transaction. Given the artificiality of par value, the modern trend in state law is to eliminate the concept altogether or to make its use discretionary. While the requirement of a minimum initial capital, such as $500, for corporations has been eliminated in many states, the level of capitalization is still important, since an undercapitalized company (one without adequate resources to operate) may leave its shareholders with some personal liability. Since one of the traditional advantages of the corporate form as a separate legal entity is to enable investors to limit their liability to the extent of their investment in the company, such a disregard of the corporate form can be truly devastating. Always make sure that all corporate formalities have been observed by the seller or you'll regret it later!

16

STOCK PURCHASE: LEGAL REVIEW (Part IV)

Most operators of incorporated small businesses have a corporate kit containing a corporate records book with separate sections for the articles, bylaws, minutes, share certificates and stock transfer ledger, and a place for the individualized corporate seal. This key analyzes the contents of a typical share certificate.

The minutes of the organizational meeting of the board should document not only adoption of the corporate seal but the share certificates and the share transfer book; a specimen share certificate should be appended to the minutes. The actual shares are numbered consecutively (e.g., 1 to 15), with the number of the certificate, imprinted in the upper left portion of the certificate, corresponding to the number on the stub which is attached to the share or is on a separate page. In the upper center of the certificate appears the phrase, "incorporated under the laws of the state of _____ "; in the upper right of the certificate, the number of shares actually issued to the shareholder is entered.

The body of the certificate shows the corporate name and, beneath that, the number of shares authorized, such as 10,000 common shares, $1.00 par value. This means that unless the corporate articles are amended, only $10,000 worth of shares at par value can be issued and outstanding. What matters for control of a corporation, of course, is the proportion of shares you own, not the absolute number.

The body of the certificate states something to the effect that "This certifies that _____

(name of shareholder) is the registered Holder of
_____ (number of shares) shares of the
Capital Stock of _____ (the
name of the corporation), fully paid and non-assessable
transferable only on the books of the Corporation by the
holder hereof in person or by Attorney upon surrender
of this Certificate properly endorsed."

At the bottom of the certificate, the corporate seal
should be impressed on the certificate, and the president
and secretary should sign, with their names printed or
typed beneath.

A few states, such as Florida, require that a documentary stamp tax be paid when the shares are issued
and at the time of any subsequent sale. The stamps must
be purchased from the state department of revenue and
physically cancelled to prevent them being used again in
a subsequent transaction. A valid transfer also requires
both the delivery and the endorsement of the certificate
by the registered owner. If a certificate is not delivered
as promised, the buyer can either compel delivery or
demand damages. If a certificate is delivered but not
properly endorsed, the corporation may not recognize
the transaction, but the transfer between buyer and seller
may still be effective.

The actual endorsement is generally accomplished by
completing the reverse side of the share certificate, although sometimes a separate stock power is used for this
purpose. The endorsement language states, "For Value
Received (indicating that consideration is present),
_____ (transferor) hereby sells, assigns, and
transfers unto _____ , _____ (specify purchaser and number of shares transferred), represented
by the within certificate, and do hereby irrevocably constitute and appoint _____ (specify name) Attorney to transfer the said Shares on the books of the
within named Corporation with full power of substitution
in the premises."

The endorsement must be signed and dated by the
selling shareholder and must be witnessed. There should
be a place on the endorsement for the social security

number of the buyer. On occasion, shares of stock, even in closely-held corporations, are held in trust, in joint tenancy, or in some other ownership capacity; thus, special care must be exercised in endorsing or issuing such shares to ensure that they are properly titled.

Assuming that the endorsement has been properly executed, the certificate must be delivered to the corporate secretary, who pastes the returned certificate in the corporate book in the place from which it had been removed. Before issuing a new certificate and recording the transaction in the transfer ledger, the secretary should demand evidence that the seller has fully complied with any applicable securities laws. A transfer of a business via a stock sale is considered to be a sale of a security so that the seller must produce either a no-action letter rendered from the SEC and the securities division of the seller's state of residence, or, more likely, an opinion letter from the seller's lawyer establishing the legality of the transaction.

17

STOCK PURCHASE: LEGAL REVIEW (Part V)

Selling shareholders may not appreciate the importance of the stub attached to the certificate (or sometimes on a separate page) and the transfer ledger. Both are extremely important for record keeping purposes and are considered here.

The stub should always remain in the corporate records book. In the upper left of the stub, next to the certificate number, is written the number of shares issued, to whom they were issued, and on what date. Any transfer of the shares is noted in the middle of the stub, where the name of the original owner, the date of transfer, the number of the original certificate, the number of original shares, and the number of shares transferred are recorded. A valid transfer must be recorded in the corporate records, and the old certificate must be cancelled and a new certificate issued.

In the upper right portion of the stub, there is a place to indicate that the transferee did in fact receive the certificate for the specified number of shares on the particular date. The stock transfer ledger closely tracks the information contained on the stub; that is, the shareholders are listed alphabetically, along with the place of the shareholder's residence, the time the shareholder became owner, and information concerning the certificate issued, such as the certificate number and number of shares.

The ledger also includes the name of the seller, the amount paid for the shares, the date of transfer of the shares, to whom the shares were transferred, and information concerning the certificate surrendered. The ledger also reflects the net number of shares held after the transfer and the value of any stock transfer tax affixed.

Thus, the share transfer ledger is used to record the issuance and subsequent transfer of stock. Your attorney should be able to account for the history of every share issued by the corporation.

In sum, record keeping is just as important for a small corporation as for a giant corporation using the services of a transfer agent. If the seller of shares claims that the shares were lost or stolen, your attorney should verify that proper procedures were followed to replace them. For this purpose, the Uniform Commercial Code in most states governs the replacement of lost, apparently destroyed, and wrongfully taken certificates representing securities and debt. Sometimes, other laws may apply as well. Note that the Replacement of shares may require the holder to post a bond adequate to indemnify the corporation if the missing shares are subsequently sold.

18

STOCK PURCHASE:
LEGAL REVIEW
(Part VI)

This key considers an important role of the seller's attorney in connection with the sale of stock of a small business: the review of the corporate documents and their possible updating.

Unfortunately, owners of small corporations often have had little guidance from their attorneys over the years, and their corporate (not necessarily their financial) records may be in poor shape and need considerable work prior to closing. Often, little has been done to keep the records current since the organizational meetings were held, and the required minutes have not been maintained. Frequently, the organizational meetings were not even held and shares never issued much less any annual meetings of the shareholders and directors held. In the most extreme cases, the corporate owners have not even bothered to file the required annual report with the department of state's office, pay the appropriate fees, or advise the department of state of a change of registered agent or office and have thereby triggered the involuntarily dissolution of the corporation.

Dissolution, whether voluntary or involuntary, is the termination of a corporation's status as a legal entity. State statutes outline the procedures for voluntary dissolution. An involuntary dissolution may be effected by either the individual shareholders or directors or the state.

In the latter case, generally, a corporation may not be involuntarily dissolved unless the department of state's office first gives notice of the proposed dissolution along with the reason(s) for the action. In addition, the corporation must have failed to correct the reasons for the proposed dissolution; by giving notice, the state grants those owners who have committed an inadvertent mistake, such as failing to file the annual report, additional time to comply.

Assuming that the corporation has been involuntarily dissolved and the owners now wish to sell the stock, what can be done? Subject to state law, the corporation may be able to apply for reinstatement by filing the annual report, and paying the appropriate fees and complying with other statutory formalities.

Generally, if the corporation is able to qualify for reinstatement, the corporate existence will be deemed to have continued without interruption from the date of dissolution, although this does not affect the personal liability of the directors, officers, and others resulting from actions taken by them for the period of time between dissolution and reinstatement.

Regardless of whether the corporation's status was dissolved and subsequently reinstated, if the corporate record keeping has been poor, it will be necessary for the seller's attorney to bring the records current before the closing date. There are various theories on how to accomplish this, but fabricating and backdating minutes is always an unacceptable solution. Any decent solution must deal frontally with the problem at a properly convened meeting at which newly-proposed minutes are proposed and adopted and then placed in the corporate record book. The precise answer depends on the problem at hand. If meetings were held but no minutes were maintained, the solution is for the corporate counsel to attempt to reconstruct the minutes and then to state at a so called "housekeeping" meeting that the board has examined the reconstructed minutes and after discussing them, agreed that the information they contain accurately reflects action taken on or about the various dates indicated. Upon completion of this discussion, and after a motion is made, seconded, and passed, the reconstructed minutes are then adopted as the official records of the corporation and the corporate secretary is directed to incorporate them in the record book.

This approach works if the minutes were never prepared. If the problem is something else (e.g., lack of proper execution of the minutes), then a different remedy is necessary. In any event, your attorney should be closely involved. Since the problem often arises from a desire to minimize the cost of counsel in the first instance, or because of the view that such work is only for "big" companies, it may be useful to contemplate how much cheaper and easier it is to do things right the first time than it is to attempt to develop a reconstructed version later on at time of sale!

19

STOCK PURCHASE: LEGAL REVIEW (Part VII)

This key describes the stock purchase agreement, which is much simpler to prepare than an asset purchase agreement. The bulk sales act is not applicable, and there generally is no need to renegotiate the lease. Although stock purchase agreements are easy to prepare, it is possible to make errors. For example, it is crucial to remember that an S corporation may not have a corporation as a shareholder—if one is listed, you have terminated the S election, and the corporation will become a regular (C) corporation subject to all corporate taxes.

Usually, a stock purchase agreement begins with some recitals. The first recital states that the seller is the owner of _____ shares of the capital stock of XYZ corporation constituting 100 percent of the issued and outstanding shares of the common stock, par value $1.00 ("the shares"). The second recital states that the seller desires to sell those shares to the buyer, and the buyer desires to purchase them. If the stock purchase agreement is combined with a noncompete agreement, a third recital might state that the seller agrees not to compete with the buyer for a specified period of time in a particular geographic area.

The consideration paid for the shares is entered in the section entitled purchase price. In the case of closely-held corporations, where there is no established market for the shares, the shares are generally valued based on a figure such as the net value of the assets at time of closing.

Stock purchase agreements may contain warranties, representations, and covenants. Although the term representation applies only to an existing fact, a warranty can also apply to something in the future; thus, something expected to be true at the time of closing can be either generally a warranty or a condition for closing. A covenant, the third form of assurance, is an agreement either to do or not to do something—classic examples are the covenant not to compete and the covenant not to sue.

Two kinds of warranties apply to stock transfers: warranties respecting the shares being transferred and warranties respecting the corporation itself. As regards the former, the seller may warrant that he or she has and will deliver good title to the shares free of any pledges or other liens, that the shares are fully paid for and non-assessable, that there are no proxies or other assignments of voting rights, and that the shares owned by the seller represent some percentage of the outstanding shares of the corporation. Your attorney should ask to see the corporate record kit and other corporate documents to determine if shares of stock were actually issued to the selling shareholder, if the shareholder does own the percentage of outstanding shares that he or she claims to own, whether all shares can be accounted for, whether any proxies are outstanding, and whether any shares have been pledged.

Your attorney will also want to know about any restrictions on transferability that may be on the share certificates themselves. Generally, such a restriction will make reference to a stock transfer agreement as follows: "The transfer of these securities is restricted by an agreement, a copy of which is on file at the office of the Corporation. The Corporation will furnish to any stockholder upon request and without charge a full statement of such restrictions." Restrictions on transferability may mean that you cannot buy the stock, or can buy it only under certain circumstances.

Many of these warranties are similar to those used in asset purchase agreements, stating, for example, that the corporation is in good standing, has good title to all of the assets, is involved in no known legal proceedings, threatened or pending, and has paid all taxes that are owed. The seller should always include a representation that the financial statements attached to the agreement were accurate as of their date of preparation and that no changes have occurred since. Sometimes, the agreement refers to other returns or financial statements (e.g., seller warrants sales to be $＿＿＿＿ as per the 1990 sales tax return.)

The next section describes conditions precedent to closing (conditions that must be met before closing can take place). For example, the seller usually warrants that there have been no adverse changes in the seller's legal, business, or financial condition and that any necessary consents or approvals have been obtained. Often a condition precedent will be that the seller be released from any existing personal guarantees and that the buyer offer a substitute personal guarantee.

The rest of the stock purchase agreement contains many of the clauses common to the asset purchase agreement, such as the closing date, as well as clauses designed to meet particular circumstances. (e.g., referring to the licenses of the seller and attaching the same to the agreement.) Like an asset purchase agreement, stock purchase agreements usually go through several drafts before being approved; even then, it is usually necessary to make some last-minute changes at the closing. Just make sure that all changes are marked legibly and initialed and that all pages are numbered and initialed by all parties to avoid a possible substitution later on.

20

THE ASSET PURCHASE

This key presents an overview of the asset purchase agreement. Such agreements vary in complexity, but all usually include the following terms:

1. **Parties and Recitals.** This introductory section clarifies who the parties are, including any broker participating in the transaction, and, if buyer and/or seller are incorporated, those individuals who stand behind the agreement. For example, the seller typically makes a number of representations, warranties, and covenants in the agreement and agrees to indemnify the buyer for any damages resulting from any misrepresentations. If the seller is a corporation and that corporation is dissolved after the assets are conveyed, the buyer is in a weak position. Therefore, the buyer should require that the shareholders of the selling corporation be personally bound for any representations made.

   After the parties to the sale are identified, the intent of the parties respecting any lease is set forth. (e.g., "the parties desire that the buyer purchase the assets of the business known as _____ and that the buyer assume the existing lease of the seller, or, in the alternative, to enter into a new lease with the landlord.")

2. **Purchase of assets.** This clause lists the specific assets being transferred (fixed assets, leasehold interest, customer lists, contract rights, telephone number, etc.). It may refer to a schedule or exhibit that presents the information in greater detail, including such information as the make and model,

year of purchase, and serial number. The name of the business is generally listed separately as an asset with a notation that the buyer has the exclusive right to register the name as a fictitious name. (You should check with your lawyer regarding "doing business as" or "DBA" requirements—the failure to comply with this statute can affect your ability to maintain or even defend a suit and can have other repercussions.) The "purchase of assets" clause is broadly written, and any items not included in the sale should be clearly spelled out; thus, this clause might state that the sale of the business "shall not include accounts receivable, bank accounts, or cash." The clause may also state that the transfer of any asset is subject to the terms and conditions of the agreement and that the "seller shall execute such documents as are reasonably required by the buyer to effectuate transfer of assets, including but not limited to, bills of sale absolute and contingent." This last point is important, since the buy-sell agreement is not self-executing—that is, signing the agreement does not put title to the various assets in the buyer's name. At the closing, the parties need to execute a bill of sale to convey the bulk of the assets, with the remainder, such as the lease, conveyed through assignment.

3. **Purchase price and terms.** The price paid for the business, although generally a fixed amount, is sometimes contingent in whole or in part on the commissions, earnings, or volume of the business. Sometimes, a fixed price is subject to an adjustment—for example, the fixed price might be $200,000 plus the dollar level of inventory as of the closing date. The price may be paid in a lump sum or in installments. The terms of financing should be clearly stated in the purchase agreement and, in greater detail, in the promissory note, security agreement, or other instruments. In certain cases, the purchase price consists of shares of stock

of the buyer or other assets. Any cash deposits that have been made with the escrow agent, whose rights and responsibilities are set forth in a clause entitled "escrow," are applied against the purchase price at closing; be sure you understand whether the deposit is refundable or nonrefundable and what actions may trigger forfeiture of the deposit. A final section of this clause, so-called prorations and adjustments, clarifies how various expenses previously incurred by the seller are to be treated; for example, the security deposit paid by the seller under the existing lease should be credited to the seller at time of closing. Each item subject to allocation, such as rent, utilities, and personal property taxes, should be addressed here.

4. **Bulk Sales Act.** Under state law, a specified number of days must pass before an asset-based deal can be closed. This clause states the obligations of buyer and seller and what documents, such as a creditor's affidavit, must be executed. To ensure that the seller's creditors have been paid, the buyer should deliver to the seller, at the closing, checks payable to the creditors, with the payments to be deducted from the purchase price, unless, prior to the closing date, the seller has delivered to the buyer acceptable written releases or waivers by all or any of the creditors. (For more on the bulk sales act, see Key 21.)

5. **Closing.** This clause states the place of closing—generally a lawyer's office—and the time of closing. Although buyers and sellers frequently think in terms of a solitary closing date—the last day of ownership by the seller—there is often a separate occupancy date, at which time buyer occupies and takes over the business, and inventory closing date, on which the buyer takes over the inventory, and accounting closing date, on which the seller's books are actually closed. This is the case since the purchase price often hinges on the date when the price is finally determined by the accountants

and any "temporary notes payable" to the seller become "permanent notes payable."

6. **Instruments of conveyance and transfer.** This clause stipulates that, at the closing, certain instruments must be executed and delivered. These include the bill of sale, the closing statement, the creditor's affidavit, the assignment of the lease, the promissory note and security agreement, and any other instruments of conveyance necessary to transfer to the buyer good and marketable title to the assets and anything else included in the sale.

7. **Representations of seller.** This clause includes those representations upon which the buyer is relying in deciding to go through with the deal. Generally, warranties and covenants of the seller are set forth separately from the representations. Typically, the representations clause contains both boilerplate (standard) and tailor-made representations. The latter are important because they force the parties and their counsel to assess carefully the legal, financial, and other aspects of the transaction.

There can be a considerable delay between the date the agreement is executed and the closing, so a well-crafted agreement will state that the representations made must be true and correct at the time of closing as well as at the time the agreement is signed. This means that if a materially adverse change occurs prior to closing, the buyer has valid grounds on which to call off the deal. Moreover, a well-drafted agreement will go a step further, providing that the representations will survive the closing and thus the buyer will have the right to sue for breach of contract (or fraud, if applicable), if the representations should turn out to be incorrect.

In the event any deficiencies are discovered prior to the closing date, the agreement generally provides that a corresponding amount is to be deducted from the purchase price. There should also be a proviso that for any deficiencies discovered after the closing date, the seller shall, upon written demand by the buyer, deliver to the buyer the full amount due, together with any interest and penalties within a specific period.

8. **Representations by the buyer.** Although the buyer's representations are not as detailed as those of the seller, the seller does want to be assured that the buyer is capable of closing the deal. Thus, the buyer represents that he or she is ready, willing, and able to close the transaction; that he or she has the full right, power, legal capacity, and authority to perform his or her obligations under the agreement, that he or she has the financial ability to accomplish the purchase, and so on. If the seller is providing financing, there will be a representation that the assets of the business will be used as security for the promissory note and that the buyer will provide to the seller notice of any event that would materially and adversely affect that security.

9. **Indemnification.** This is the mechanism for implementing the representations, warranties and covenants included in the other sections, and it must be drawn with care. For example, what will be the sanction for a seller misrepresentation—does the seller just have to make the buyer whole or does it constitute grounds for rescission of the whole contract. Further, is there any dollar limit on the amount to be indemnified? If not, a seller could be liable to a buyer for an amount greatly in excess of the purchase price. Generally, this clause states that in the event of a breach by the seller, the seller will indemnify and hold the buyer harmless from any cost, liability, or expense, and that the buyer shall have the right to set off any such costs, liabilities, or expenses against all sums payable to the seller.

Next, the clause states that, in the event of a third-party (someone other than the buyer and the seller) claim, the seller has the right to defend against the claim provided the seller has demonstrated to the buyer's satisfaction that he or she will be able to pay or otherwise satisfy the indemnification obligations. Next, the buyer and seller agree, on demand, to promptly indemnify the other from, and reimburse the other for, any damages incurred by the other after the closing date that results from any misrepresentations or any failure to perform any obligation or duty required by the agreements.

10. **Conditions precedent to closing.** Since there will be a gap in time between the date the agreement is executed and the closing, there must be a clause to cover what is to occur during that gap. For example, from and after the date of execution of the agreement until the closing, the seller should agree to operate the business in substantially the same manner as before, to use his or her best efforts to maintain and preserve the business intact, and to keep the business in good operating condition, ordinary wear and tear excepted.

Further, it should be agreed that any required consent from any lessor, lender, mortgagee, payee or secured parties must be obtained for closing to take place. Another condition that must be met for closing to occur is that there must be "no material adverse changes in the financial or business condition of the seller, including casualty losses, whether or not insured." Finally, this paragraph should state that no governmental inquiry shall have been asserted, threatened, or instituted that might adversely affect the business or assets of the seller.

11. **Training after closing.** This clause states that for an agreed-upon period of time immediately following the closing, the seller shall use his or her best efforts to assist and train the buyer in the operation and management of the business and to facilitate the orderly transition of the business.

Specifics should be spelled out. This clause generally goes on to say that following the interval, the seller will render assistance to the buyer as agreed on, on a compensated basis. Also, in this clause, the buyer agrees to reimburse the seller for all expenses reasonably incurred in providing these services, as long as written approval for these expenses has been first obtained from the buyer.

12. **Covenant not to compete.** This clause states that the seller will not conduct, establish, or be engaged in a competitive business for a specified geographic area and period of time following the closing, and that the buyer can seek injunctive and other relief to enforce this covenant. Generally, the clause contains a sentence stating that the covenant shall be construed as an agreement independent of any other provision in this agreement and shall not be invalidated by the existence of any claim or cause of action. This means that the presence of some other claim does not excuse the parties from being bound under the covenant.

13. **Brokerage.** This clause protects the broker's commission and starts by stating that the broker is the only one the buyer and seller have dealt with and that the buyer and seller agree to indemnify each other and the broker for any damages arising out of a claim for commission by some other broker. The clause then says that by the execution of the agreement, the brokerage commission has been fully earned and that both buyer and seller agree to pay any fees and costs necessary to collect that commission. The amount of the commission due the broker must be specified; sometimes a minimum fee is also stated.

14. **Miscellaneous clauses.** The agreement may also contain a number of miscellaneous clauses, many of which are common to all business transfer agreements. For example, there may be a clause relating to "successors and assigns" that states that the provisions of the agreement will insure to the ben-

efit of and bind the successors and assigns of the parties and their executors, administrators, heirs, successors, and assigns. This means that the estates of the parties are bound by the agreement.

It is your obligation to ask questions of your advisers regarding the various terms and conditions in the agreement and to suggest any necessary changes. Sometimes, a buyer or seller finds out the hard way the importance of a particular sentence buried in the agreement months or even years after the agreement's execution.

21

BULK SALES ACT

Most states have enacted some version of the bulk transfer statute (Article 6 of the Federal Uniform Commercial Code). If an acquisition is an asset acquisition (not a stock sale), if a substantial portion of the seller's inventory or equipment is being transferred, and if the buyer is not assuming the seller's liabilities, the buyer must comply with this statute in the state where the assets are located. Failure to do so will cause the assets to be subject to the claims of the seller's creditors even after title has passed to the buyer.

The rationale of this statute is to prevent business owners from secretly conveying the bulk of their business assets to others in order to avoid creditor claims. Some states, like Florida, not only require that the creditors be informed of the transfer but impose an obligation on the buyer to ensure that the proceeds of the sale are actually used to pay off the debts of the former business.

Fortunately, it is relatively easy to comply with the statute. The buyer must obtain an affidavit from the seller containing a complete list of the seller's creditors and the amounts owed to each. The buyer must then send a timely notice of the planned transfer to the creditors. Generally, this notice must be furnished at least ten days before the transfer of the property or the payment, and must be given to all known creditors, including all those identified on the list of creditors and those known to the buyer. The notice must state that a bulk transfer is to be made, identify the transferor (seller) and the transferee (buyer), list their addresses, and state whether the debts of the transferor will be paid. In certain states, if the debts are not to be deposited into an escrow account, other requirements must be met.

The transferor must attest to the accuracy of the list of creditors; in some states, making false statements is a criminal offense. If the transferor indicates that there are no creditors, an affidavit to that effect must be prepared. For the buyer's protection, however, the buyer's attorney should check public records for the existence of possible creditors, retain a portion of the purchase price in the event creditors' claims have to be satisfied, and have the right to deduct from purchase payments (if the seller is providing financing) any creditors' claims that need to be satisfied.

Although bulk sales laws vary among the states, the California law is fairly typical. Under California law, if the business being sold is a bakery, cafe or restaurant, garage, or cleaner and dyer, or if the principal business is the sale of merchandise, the seller must prepare and publish a Notice to Creditors of Bulk Transfer in the judicial district in which the property being sold is located and, if different, in the judicial district where the chief executive office of the business is situated.

Under California law, the required publication must be completed at least 12 business days before the date the property is transferred to the new owner. Copies of the notice must also be filed with the County Recorder and the County Tax Collector at least 12 business days before the sale is to be closed in the counties where the property is located.

The bulk sales law also applies if you are incorporating an existing business. If you buy the assets of an existing business individually and then incorporate the business, you may need to satisfy the bulk sales act twice. Fortunately, state law may provide an exemption in such cases. In Florida, for example, there is an exemption if:

1. the assets of the prior business are transferred to a new business organized to take over and continue the prior business
2. the new enterprise assumes all the debts of the transferor
3. the transferors receive nothing from the transaction

except an interest in the new enterprise that has lower priority than the claims of creditors

4. public notice of the sale of the assets of the prior business is given.

The incorporation of an existing business should quality under the first test. To meet the second test, the corporation must assume prior business debts; thus, an offer to transfer the business assets to the newly-formed corporation must also cover business liabilities. If the former owners receive preferred stock or anything of value beyond shares of common stock, the third test will not be met. The fourth requirement can be satisfied through publication of an advertisement for two consecutive weeks in a newspaper of general circulation. As is the case with the bulk sales act generally, the two-week notice requirement must be met before the assets of the prior business can be transferred to the corporation and shares of stock issued. Although this notice is the only requirement imposed under Florida law, clearly it would be better practice to notify existing creditors individually of the transfer of the business to the corporation. Check the law of your own jurisdiction for details.

22

VALUING THE BUSINESS

Once you decide to sell your business, you need to value it in order to justify a proper asking price. Similarly, if you decide to buy a business, a valuation will help you determine a suitable offering price.

The standard measure of value—the price at which property changes hands between a willing buyer and willing seller, both knowledgeable of the relevant facts and neither under any compulsion to sell—implies that both sides are equally armed with the facts. This may be an erroneous assumption, however. Since the seller undoubtedly knows more about the business than the buyer and probably has revealed all conceivable information enhancing the value of the business and omitted unfavorable information, the price may be excessively high. Therefore, a wise buyer should have obtained as much information about the selling business, the seller, the industry, and the economy as a whole as possible prior to making an offer since all have a bearing on price. Further, some information can cut both ways in determining value. For example, a business in a rapidly growing community may appear to be a better buy than one in a stable area. On the other hand, the rapid growth of the area may draw new competition than can cut into sales.

Generally, pre-acquisition studies provide information on the value of a business for negotiation purposes. Of the several methods in use today, considered here are the book value method, the cost method, the liquidation value method, the market value method, the multiple of earnings method, and the capitalization of earnings methods.

The simplest way to approach valuation is the book value method. This entails taking the current book value of the company's assets and subtracting the book value of the liabilities, adjusting for any intangibles such as goodwill and deferred financing costs. A problem with the book value method and its variants is that adjustments must be made for a number of tangible and intangible assets. For example, many assets are carried at their historical cost and are therefore understated, while other items, such as bad debt reserve, are only estimates and may be understated or overstated. Moreover, different methods may be acceptable for accounting purposes but may yield different values, making it impossible to arrive at a true book value. Using any book value, particularly an unadjusted book value, represents a poor choice, especially for a company with a short or relatively unstable business history, one that has experienced labor problems, supply shortages, or other circumstances making future earnings unpredictable or one that has a sole owner who has become ill or disabled or who has left the business.

The cost method is based on the belief that the best way to set a value for a business is to determine what it would cost to replace or reproduce the items based on current costs. Inflation and the annual depreciation of capital assets generally causes the replacement value to be much higher than the book value. The problems with this method are that it fails to reflect the value of intangibles, such as goodwill and customer lists, and that it ignores the fact that certain assets would not be replaced if the company were rebuilt (e.g., a company might choose a more cost-efficient alternative to an obsolete piece of machinery). A home appraiser often gives at least two values, the replacement cost and the value based on the recent sale of comparable properties in the area (see market value method below.) Although the replacement cost method can be accurate for fairly new businesses, it is less accurate for older businesses.

The liquidation value method calculates the net amount the owner would realize if all the assets were sold and the liabilities paid. This value tends to set a floor value, but since it does not reflect the goodwill (or going concern) aspect of a business, it is of limited use.

The market value method approaches the problem by comparing the business with similar ones recently put up for sale adjusting the sales price for factors such as the age of the business and the condition of the building and equipment. This method is quite difficult to apply, except for franchised businesses, which may truly be comparable.

The next method is the multiple of earnings. Since an acquisition is made to generate earnings, it is the earnings that truly determine value, so this method has some appeal. In this method, the net profits for the prior years are averaged and then capitalized by multiplying the average by the price/earnings ratio. The result is then divided by the number of outstanding shares yielding a value par share. For example, assume that in the previous three years, profits averaged $100,000 and that the price/earnings ratio is 8; if the p/e ratio is 8, the value of the company should be $800,000, and if 1000 shares are outstanding, the value per share should be $80. The problem with this method (or any method incorporating earnings) is possible inaccuracies in reported income and expense. This problem may be caused by a lack of good records, but even good records may not present a fair picture of the company as seen by a potential buyer. Consider, for example, an owner who has taken a salary of $90,000 when a reasonable salary under the circumstances would have been $50,000. The $40,000 is considered excess compensation; that is, a buyer who purchases the business would either pay him or herself or an outside manager $50,000. This means that expenses are overstated by $40,000 and income is understated by $40,000. Similarly, maybe the owner has been paying a son $20,000 a year for doing nothing. That's not an expense a buyer will incur if he or she acquires the business. Other items of income and expense in turn should be so normalized to reflect a realistic value. If the percentage of sales spent on advertising is too low for a business of this type, that figure may need to be increased and net income reduced; maybe the company is badly underinsured and the insurance premium needs to be doubled.

Another problem here is that you need a p/e ratio. (For closely-held corporations, securities are unlisted, so there is no set price.) Under the capitalization of earnings method, the return on investment is divided into pre-tax profits. A number of factors may affect the rate to be applied, including the nature of the business, the perceived stability of the earnings, and the risks involved, so the riskier the business, the higher the rate that must be applied. Assume that a reasonable return for one prospect is 10 percent and for another, 20 percent. In the first company, the buyer is willing to pay ten times the company's earnings, while in the latter case, the buyer is willing to pay only five times earnings. Put somewhat differently, in the first case, the buyer is demanding a ten-year payback, while in the latter case the buyer requires a payback in just five years.

A variant of the capitalization of earnings method is the excess earnings method, in which the value of the business's tangible assets is multiplied by an appropriate interest rate. The result is added to the annual salary expected from the business, and the sum, the total pretax profit, is compared to the annual profit predicted from the business. The excess is multiplied by the number of years it would have taken you to reach the same level of profitability if you had started a business from scratch; this figure is the goodwill. Adding goodwill to the value of the tangible assets, yields the value of the business as a whole.

Another variant is the discounted cash flow method, in which one selects a period of time, such as five years, and estimates the expected cash flows during a specified number of years. The valuator multiplies the flows by an appropriate interest rate and determines the present value of each flow, totals the present values of the cash flows, and arrives at the value.

In sum, there are basically three types of valuation methods in use today—asset-based valuations (such as the liquidation value method), earnings-based valuations (such as the multiple of earnings method), and hybrid methods (such as the excess earnings method, which is used by the IRS and which considers both earnings and assets). There are many other factors that affect value; a business on the verge of a breakthrough may be worth more while a business dependent on two customers may be worth less. You should keep in mind that prior to beginning the sales process, any prudent seller will have "dressed up" the business, complete with a new make-over and perhaps some revised financials. For example, it is not unusual for sellers who seek a stock sale and don't wish to convey certain assets, such as real estate, to form a new company as a subsidiary of the first and then transfer the saleable assets to the subsidiary. Similarly, the seller may have already "sold out" some of the better-valued assets and left only the "lower-grade" items in stock. The answer is to investigate as thoroughly as possible and to have an experienced business valuation expert involved in the process from early on.

23

MAKING THE OFFER

After completing the valuation of the business, it's time to develop a price complete with appropriate terms. Clearly, you expect to pay less for an all-cash deal than if the seller finances 80 percent of the purchase price; by avoiding the need for seller financing, you have effectively reduced the seller's risk of nonpayment. Other factors play a role as well, including how long the business has been on the market, how badly you want to buy the business, how badly the seller wants to sell it, how badly the seller needs money, and so forth.

The seller may take a number of approaches here. One is to say that the offer is laughable and that there are several higher offers. The seller also may take the opposite approach, saying that a pressing need for cash has led to a low asking price. What matters is not what the seller says the business is worth—what matters is what, based on the information you have gathered, you think it's worth. Invariably, the seller starts high to allow room for negotiation, you invariably start low. The seller can either accept your offer, reject it or make a counteroffer. Just make sure you set a deadline on the acceptance of the offer so there is no question about its expiration date. Expect the seller to claim that there have been other offers more favorable than yours—but if that is the case, why has one not been accepted?

It is possible that the seller may not know the true worth of the business—perhaps with a few minor changes, a new owner could greatly increase sales. More likely, the seller knows much more than the buyer and what is not being told to the buyer would diminish the company's value not increase it. You should have a basis for comparison; know, for example, what similar businesses in the area have been going for. Investigate the business thoroughly to arrive at a supportable price. One thing you should not do is to ask the broker's opinion of the company's worth. Unless you have retained the broker, the broker works for the seller, and asking the broker's opinion on price creates an awkward situation.

How much should you expect to put down? Clearly, much depends on how much can be raised, but at a minimum you should be able to put down the loan value of the assets (e.g., 80 percent of the accounts receivable); preferably, you should be able to put down the book net worth.

Assume you have decided to buy a business for $100,000, have $10,000 saved, and can raise $10,000 more from friends. That leaves $80,000 to be raised. If you go to the bank, you may pay an exorbitant interest rate and be required to repay the loan in too short a period. If, on the other hand, you borrow the $80,000 from the seller, you may receive a lower interest rate and increase the payment period. Since the seller is a small business owner and is not in the business of lending funds, and since the seller wants the deal to go through, you may get a better deal. A seller who is transferring assets will be able to take a security interest in the assets sold; if shares are being sold you can pledge your shares to the seller. The seller may ask for a personal guarantee or a pledge of some personal assets, but try to avoid this if possible. Everything's negotiable. Perhaps if you offer a higher down payment and a higher interest rate, the seller will not insist on a personal guarantee. Other sellers want not only for the buyer to sign a personal guarantee but for a cosigner to back the loan as well.

Assuming that the seller is agreeable to providing 80 percent financing (i.e., $80,000 of the $100,000 needed), over what term should repayment be made and at what interest rate? It is important that you arrive at a monthly payment that you can live with; once a monthly payment has been determined, a suitable interest rate and period can be selected. Sometimes sellers can be surprisingly flexible and creative in their financing.

Whatever terms are agreed on should be formalized in an offer to purchase or in a letter of intent. In the offer to purchase, you as the buyer offer "to purchase the assets and goodwill of the business known as _____ _____ located at, _____ _____" and state that "the purchase price shall be $_____ (including inventory) and that the down payment shall be $_____ _____." If you are going to assume existing encumbrances, the approximate amount should be stated as follows, "I will assume existing encumbrances of approximately $_____ payable at $_____ per month, which includes _____ percent interest. The balance of approximately $_____ _____ will be paid to the seller at $_____ _____ per month including _____ _____ percent interest per annum."

The offer should say that the sale will satisfy the applicable state bulk sales act, that all equipment must be in good working order, and that the seller agrees to provide training and assistance. Any contingencies (e.g., lease contingency, buyer's approval of the seller's books and records, contingent financing) should be clearly stated. When satisfied, such contingencies should be removed through the device of a contingency removal clause. A closing date should be specified and the offer should be signed and dated. Generally, the buyer attaches a deposit, and the following statement appears at the bottom of the offer: "Attached is a deposit for $_____. This check may not be cashed until the terms of this agreement have been met and is to be subtracted from the down payment. If this offer is not accepted by _____ _____ (date), or contingent financing is not obtained, or the buyer does not approve the books, records, or lease, this check is to be returned." Thus, the offer sets forth an expiration date and makes it clear under what circumstances the deposit check is to be refunded.

A "letter of intent" is often used if the parties have

reached agreement on the essential terms and conditions of a deal. It is generally accompanied by a deposit. The letter of intent gives the buyer the option to purchase for a particular period of time and, like an offer, precedes the signing of any final agreement. After identifying the parties and the option period, the letter ordinarily begins with a description of the transaction and discusses any representations, warranties, covenants, and conditions of sale. There is generally an indemnification clause, a termination clause, a deposit clause, and perhaps some miscellaneous clauses.

Let's discuss each of these in turn from the standpoint of the buyer and seller. The interest of buyer and seller in getting a decent description of the business is the same, although one may prefer a stock deal and the other an asset deal. Each should want specificity in how the purchase price is to be paid. In the representations clause, the buyer represents that he or she is willing and able to consummate the transaction, while the seller makes a number of specific representations (e.g., the existence of any pending litigation.) The seller resists making representations, the buyer insists on them. The same applies to the warranties. Affirmative/negative covenants are common in business transfers; thus, the seller might covenant not to take on additional long-term debt. The conditions precedent clause states the events that must occur for closing to take place. Examples of buyer-suggested conditions precedent are the right to inspect the books and records, to review the inventory, and to have the agreement contingent on the buyer obtaining financing. An example of a seller-suggested condition precedent is that a favorable IRS ruling on a point of tax law be obtained. The indemnification clause generally cuts both ways, with both parties agreeing to indemnify each other in the event of a breach of a representation or warranty. A breach of the agreement may also constitute grounds for termination of the agreement and this should be stated in that clause, as should any other conditions that might constitute grounds for abandoning the deal. There may be a reference to an additional deposit (if a deposit has to be given at all) due in the event the closing date is not met. From the buyer's point of view, the deposit itself should always be refundable and generate interest; the seller seeks a large, nonrefundable deposit, with the seller benefiting from any interest. Each party should sign and date the letter of intent, and the signatures should be witnessed. In some cases, neither an offer nor a letter of intent will be used, but a form purchase and sale agreement that sets forth the essential terms of the deal. In any case, a detailed agreement will be prepared eventually and should state that it supersedes any prior writings on the subject.

24

CLOSING THE DEAL

You have decided to buy a particular business and, having investigated and valued it and made an offer, you are now ready to close the deal. There will probably be a period of time between the date you sign a purchase agreement and the date of closing. The beginning of the month is a typical cut-off date. It is a good idea to make the closing period as short as possible to maintain the momentum of the deal. Buyers often want time to conduct as thorough a review as possible before committing themselves financially and emotionally; although ideally the buyer and the buyer's advisers will have conducted their due diligence work before signing the agreement, many times that has not been possible because the buyer has had only limited access to detailed financial information. Make sure there's a way to pull back from the deal if new and damaging information is found, and make the most of this opportunity to uncover any hidden liabilities requiring immediate attention.

As part of this due diligence effort, your attorney should conduct a title search on the real estate, if applicable, and look into whether there are any liens or charges against the property being acquired. (The attorney should check again after the closing to ascertain whether any new liens or encumbrances have been recorded since the last check.) The buyer should work with the seller to learn the business—what goods or services are being sold, who the good and bad employees are, what the business's accounting system is, who the prime customers are, and anything else that might help in running the business. Unless you plan to hire an experienced manager to run the business, you'll need to be able to make decisions quickly and confidently; you'll also want to ensure an orderly transition by avoiding abrupt changes, in the product pricing or features, for example.

Prior to the closing, you'll want to make sure that all of the closing documents have been prepared and all contingencies, such as the assignment of the lease, have been considered. The closing is not the time to start negotiating a new lease. You should be sure to obtain all of the necessary licenses, apply to the state liquor agency, if applicable, and put the telephone and utilities in your name. This is a place where additional liabilities sometimes turn up.

If you're buying assets and if you didn't incorporate before signing the agreement, you'll want to incorporate during the closing period, hold any organizational meetings, and obtain an employer taxpayer identifying number and sales tax number. You should obtain copies of any existing insurance policies, conduct a complete risk assessment of the business, and identify any gaps in coverage. (You may be surprised by the claims history of the seller.) You should review any existing employment agreements, union contracts, and any other agreements to be assumed in the transaction.

After doing this basic work, you'll need to bring certain items in addition to the closing. These include the lease assignment or new lease; the balance of funds to be paid the seller; a bill of sale conveying the assets; a security agreement; financing statement; franchisor approval, if applicable; state liquor license approval, if applicable; the Uniform Commercial Code (UCC) search; any corporate resolutions approving the purchase and sale; proof of bulk sales act compliance; pro-rated portions of rent, utilities, and other items; a list of fixtures and equipment; and a detailed inventory list.

The seller will also have work to do. The seller may need to update the corporate records book and hold any necessary meetings to facilitate the sale. The seller may be asked for a certified copy of incorporation in the state, a sales tax waiver, and similar documents. The seller may be asked to produce a "cold comfort letter" at closing from either an independent CPA or the seller's own accountant that indicates the extent to which the financial statements provided by the seller may be relied upon. Similarly, the seller may be asked to produce an opinion of counsel from the seller's attorney which covers not only basic matters of corporate status but more detailed matters, such as the existence of any pending or threatened litigation. The seller has to close out the books, reconcile any bank accounts, and prepare any final tax returns. The seller will need to transfer any vehicles to the new buyer—if this is covered, they may well be subject to sales tax; transfer any license, permits, and registrations covered by the agreement to the buyer; and notify any other affected parties, from employees to customers to suppliers to banks to professional advisers. The seller needs to assign any lease, distributorship, patents, or similar items and obtain payoff amounts on any secured debt. In addition, the seller will want to make sure that the utility and telephone service have been cancelled, any existing bank accounts closed, any insurance policies cancelled, any professional service contracts cancelled, and any personal guarantees made on behalf of the corporation ended.

This last point is one of the most important handled in the pre-closing phase. Although certain obligations (e.g., employment tax obligations imposed on "responsible persons" under federal law), may be difficult to shift, it is possible to be released from personally guaranteed debt if creditor approval can be obtained. Often a decision to effect a stock transfer is made with the express understanding that the seller's shareholders be released from any personal guarantees. Like a lease contingency that does not work out in the pre-closing period, the failure to be released from such guaranties may be enough either to kill the deal entirely or to convert the deal to an asset sale. (Otherwise, a financially strong shareholder, though not at fault, might be potentially liable for huge amounts after leaving the business. In some cases, it is possible to satisfy the debt prior to closing, thus eliminating the issue, but, in other cases, the seller's shareholders may be asked to stay on personally following the closing. Even with an indemnification, such an approach seems risky, especially if the obligations being covered are long-term in nature.)

Assuming that all relevant issues have been worked out, the closing usually takes place in one of the lawyer's offices. Both sides should have worked everything out in advance so the closing is essentially a signing ceremony. Any missing detail can hold up the deal. For example, the landlord may have agreed to assign the lease but have changed his mind at the end. Although some problems at closing that arise cannot be foreseen, many are preventable; both parties, who have invested so much in closing the deal, should commit enough resources to ensure that as many potential snags as possible are cleared up. This paves the way not only for a smoother closing but for a more cordial environment in the post-closing period. As a buyer, you will quickly see that the seller's help can be invaluable in many areas; as a seller, it is in your interest to have the buyer succeed, especially if the bulk of the financing is seller financed. Although the seller will soon be out of the picture, the parting should be on a friendly cooperative basis.

25

FINANCING THE ACQUISITION: OVERVIEW

This is the first of six keys dealing with financing the proposed purchase of an existing business. This key presents an overview of the process; succeeding keys focus on long-term financing, intermediate-term financing, short-term financing, SBA loans, and seller financing.

In order to obtain financing, you will probably need to prepare a business plan that establishes how much financing is actually needed and gives the lender some assurance that the loan will be repaid. A business plan is also useful if you plan to obtain additional capital, since it includes an analysis of earnings potential for prospective investors.

Typically, a business plan contains several sections, including a description of the business concept, a discussion of market considerations, management, financial performance, financing and the various phases of the plan. The plan should address the sources and uses of funds; thus, a plan might call for $155,000 of funds for a new business, broken down as follows: purchase of the assets, $95,000; purchase of inventory, $40,000; and initial working capital, $20,000. (Working capital is needed to finance start-up costs, such as deposits for telephone, utilities, and rent.) For purposes of this example, assume the entrepreneur has $30,000 for a down payment, can obtain $105,000 in financing from the seller, and needs $20,000 from the bank in the form of a short-term loan.

The buyer proposes to pay the seller $105,000 over a ten-year period based on an interest rate of 10 percent annum, or $1387.59 per month. The seller would like a shorter payback period, perhaps five years. Buyer and seller then agree that the monthly payments will be based on a ten-year amortization with a balloon payment due after the fifth year (i.e., the buyer must pay $65,307.09 on the 61st payment). The buyer can raise the funds either by negotiating a new payment plan with the seller or from another source; by then, the buyer may have a track record sufficient from which to seek funds.

Not surprisingly, most buyers prefer as long an amortization period as possible; note, though, that debt service costs generally should not exceed 25 percent of the returns from a business. Some sellers, finding that an all-cash deal is not feasible, assume that they will be able to sell the note to some wealthy investor and obtain the cash funds right away. Although such persons (and entities) do exist and can sometimes be found through newspaper advertising, for example, they do require that the note be substantially discounted and often impose special conditions on the debt. It is far better to find out if such an investor is available and interested before the deal is done than to wait until after the fact. Buyers, of course, prefer to make the notes non-negotiable. This helps preserve their position in the event liabilities are subsequently discovered.

26

FINANCING THE ACQUISITION: LONG TERM

This key describes the two principal sources of long-term financing (financing with a term of more than five years): equity and debt financing. The other possibility—internal sources of funds such as retained earnings, asset reductions, or the sale of assets not essential to the business—is not considered here.

Those who provide the equity financing are the owners of the business and may include the buyer, family, friends, and others who have agreed to risk their capital in the business. It may be necessary to tap into your savings, the equity in your home, and other sources, in order to come up with the down payment for acquiring a business. Before doing so, however, you should take into account the high failure rate among new businesses, many of which are attributable to undercapitalization. If you do not have sufficient funds to get through the tough start-up period, then all your effort may be for naught.

There are many advantages to equity financing. First, equity increases a company's net worth and creditworthiness by increasing its assets without a corresponding increase in liabilities. Second, equity financing is permanent capital; it does not require repayment and imposes no set charges that directly affect business operations. Another, often-overlooked, advantage of equity financing is that, unlike banks and other commercial lenders that sometimes require a personal guarantee, the pledge of personal collateral, and perhaps even a co-signer, equity investors make no such demands.

Equity financing has its disadvantages. First, equity

financing becomes expensive compared to debt financing when a business does well. Giving a "money person" a 50 percent share for a $100,000 contribution to capital may seem like a great idea at the time you're starting the business but may seem like a terrible idea in retrospect when the corporation is worth $10 million. Second, outside creditors share equally any remaining assets if the business is liquidated. Although shareholder-creditor loans must ordinarily be satisfied before holders of common stock receive any settlements, if the corporation was undercapitalized when formed, the courts may determine it to be unfair for a controlling shareholder to participate equally with the outside creditors (i.e., the court will subordinate the claims of the shareholder creditors to the claims of the outside creditors.)

The conventional form of long-term financing for any new business is debt. A mortgage is simply a grant by the borrower known as the mortgagor, to a lender, known as the mortgagee, that gives the lender priority in a particular asset such as a building. This means that if the debtor defaults on a loan, the creditor holding the mortgage is permitted to force the sale of the asset pledged as security through a procedure known as foreclosure. Proceeds of the sale go to the holder of the first mortgage before any other creditors are paid.

Generally, the mortgage holder—the lender—looks at the track record of a prospective borrower before making any loan. The lender uses several financial ratios to evaluate the borrower's creditworthiness. Subject to industry variations, if the borrower's total debt represents more than 200 to 300 percent of net worth or if long-term debt itself exceeds net worth, the business may be deemed excessively leveraged; such a high level of debt leaves a small cushion if something goes wrong. Beyond financial considerations, the lender wants to be sure that the debtor has good professional advice and that the business is being managed by an experienced person.

The terms of the loan vary from deal to deal. Although loan terms are usually no more than 20 to 25 years, they may be for a much shorter period than that. The maximum level of financing available varies but is generally approximately three quarters of the appraised value of the building and land offered as security.

Loans are generally paid off on a monthly basis, with each payment a combination of interest and principal. An amortization schedule determines the payments; the term amortization rate refers to the speed with which the principal of the loan is paid off.

Most loans do not permit early prepayment for several years; if prepayment is allowed, there may be a penalty. The purpose of this policy is to discourage the debtor from trading in the old mortgage if interest rates drop after the loan agreement is signed. Conversely, the loan agreement may contain a call provision allowing the lender, after a specified period of time, to ask for complete repayment of the loan, which it may choose to do if interest rates rise. If this occurs, lender and debtor may renegotiate a new mortgage—at the new, higher rate.

Numerous other terms may be contained in the agreement. The lender may require equity participation—a block of stock—in the business or up-front fees, points, or a bonus. Whatever it's called, the effect is the same: to raise the interest rate on the debt.

Finally, the lender may request a personal guarantee from the debtor. This means that even if the business is incorporated, the creditors can reach beyond the corporate assets to the borrower's personal assets to seek repayment of the loan. (This is separate and distinct from attempts by creditors to pierce the corporate veil as a result of commingling corporate with personal assets, failing to hold corporate meetings, etc.). It is important once the underlying loan gets paid off that a release from the personal guarantee be obtained; if the business is sold via a stock transfer, the selling shareholder should seek a release as well.

Debt financing has several advantages. From the standpoint of the investor, debt offers less risk because it receives higher priority than equity if the company is liquidated. From the corporation's point of view, unlike the dividend payments, the interest payment is tax deductible. Debt securities are cost-effective because they pay a lower rate of interest than the fixed dividend rate payable on preferred shares; they also provide the opportunity for the company to obtain additional funds on the basis of higher returns without creating increased ownership interest. For franchised businesses, the fact of being a franchise sometimes results in lower interest rates than apply to similar, nonfranchised businesses, depending on the location and the point in the business's life when the borrowing takes place.

There are disadvantages associated with debt financing, too. First, a corporation that is heavily leveraged may find it hard to obtain additional financing and credit. Second, the debt payments can burden the business; unlike the payment of dividends, which is discretionary, the failure to make a required payment to a creditor constitutes a default for which the creditor has immediate remedies available to it. Further, if the corporation is undercapitalized (i.e., the initial investment of capital by the shareholders is inadequate for the purpose of operating the business in light of the economic needs and risks of the business), the IRS may classify otherwise deductible interest payments to shareholders as nondeductible constructive dividends.

In sum, although partial financing may be available from banks, especially if you are seeking a home-equity loan, many banks are reluctant to get involved in long-term financing unless real estate or government assistance is available. The answer may be for the buyer to raise the purchase price through the use of personal savings, life insurance cash values, loans from family, friends, and other interested parties, and perhaps through seller financing.

27

FINANCING THE ACQUISITION: INTERMEDIATE TERM

There are two major types of intermediate-term financing: term loans and installment financing.

Intermediate-term loans that run for from one to five years, like short-loans (see Key 28), are generally obtained from banks, but they have a different purpose. Intermediate-term loans are often used to cover the purchase of inventory, furniture, fixtures, equipment, and similar items, and perhaps to replace long-term debt that carries a higher rate of interest. Typically, term loans are repaid in installments over the life of the loan and carry an interest rate a bit higher than that on short-term loans. Intermediate-term loans may permit repayment without penalty.

Installment financing is used for the purchase of various kinds of equipment and fixtures when a term loan may not be possible; for example, a supplier may act as an intermediary between a commercial finance company and a debtor to arrange the financing. Such loans generally entail a substantial down payment and have a relatively high interest rate. They are often secured by a chattel mortgage on the assets financed; the chattel mortgage is generally recorded and permits the lender to sell the pledged assets if default occurs. Alternatively, such a loan can be done with a conditional sales contract. In such case, the lender retains title to the assets until all of the terms of the contract have been satisfied.

28

FINANCING THE ACQUISITION: SHORT TERM

Most bank lending involves short-term loans that are used to meet the operational needs of businesses and have terms of less than one year. Most are revolving loans in which the proceeds are used to pay for manufacturing expenses, processing expenses, the purchase of inventory, and similar objectives and the loan is repaid when the business cycle is completed through customer payment. When additional sales in turn produce new accounts receivable, then new revolving loans may be needed.

The most basic form of short-term financing is trade credit. An existing business has a credit rating that can be obtained from the major credit reporting services. If you buy the stock of the company, you can benefit from that credit rating; if you buy the assets of the company, the credit reporting services may themselves solicit from you the names of several vendors who can give the new business a favorable report. It is always wise to stay on good terms with your suppliers.

In deciding whether to extend credit to you after you acquire the business, suppliers will ask you to complete a detailed credit application. They may contact your banker, ask for numerous references, and contact others in the business who have dealt with you in the past. They may pay you a personal visit and ask for detailed information ranging from corporation and financial data to the names and addresses of your professional advisers to a description of the physical plant and the local economy.

Expect the supplier to continually update this information.

Based on its investigation, the supplier will offer you one of three credit options: cash on delivery (COD), cash discount, or "no cash discount."

Cash on delivery offers no vendor financing at all; for example, a supplier of food products might demand immediate payment and instruct the drivers not to deliver the goods if payment is not received.

Cash discount means that you will be allowed a specified period of time, such as 30 days, to make payment. If you pay earlier than required, you will receive a discount. For example, the phrase "2/10 net 30" means that payment is required within 30 days, but if you pay within ten days, you will receive a 2 percent discount. The purpose of such a policy is to encourage early payment.

Ignoring such a discount can be costly. For example, if you make a $10,000 purchase under the terms just described and pay within the ten-day period, your cost will be only $9800. (From an accounting standpoint, one debits accounts payable in the amount of $10,000, credits cash in the amount of $9800, and credits purchase discount in the amount of $200.) If you don't take the discount, you retain use of the funds for an additional twenty days, but at an effective cost of 37.2 percent, computed as follows: $200/$9800 × 365/20 = 37.2 percent.

No cash discount means that full payment is required within a specified number of days after the goods are delivered. This may not sound like a great deal, but if you begin to delay payment, you may find yourself converted to a COD customer overnight. Regardless of the payment arrangement, you should never agree to a personal guarantee if you can avoid it since you will have cosigned the debt.

Short-term loans are generally negotiated for a specified period of time such as 30 or 60 days and are usually payable in installments or in a lump sum. Each loan is covered by a promissory note stating the terms of the loan, including the amount borrowed, the interest rate, and the manner of repayment. The interest rate charged depends on competitive conditions and your credit rating and may be given at a stated annual rate that differs from the effective rate if the loan is discounted (the process by which interest is deducted in advance on a loan). For example, assume a $10,000 loan is taken out at the beginning of a year, to be repaid at the end of a year at a discount rate of 12 percent. The debtor receives $8800 (i.e., $1,000 minus $1200 interest) but is required to repay $10,000 at the end of the year. This means that the effective interest rate is $1200/$8800 or 13.6 percent.

The effective interest rate differs from the stated interest rate if the loan is payable in installments over the life of the loan rather than at the end of the loan period. Regardless of the type of loan involved, it is important to determine the true, effective interest rate applicable to the loan.

Unsecured loans on which no collateral is necessary, are available only to borrowers of the highest standing; generally, such borrowers receive favorable interest rates on the loan since their credit standing is strong enough to reduce the probability of a loan default. The two major categories of unsecured loans are business-cycle loans (a form of short-term loan) and lines of credit, which are more commonly used by borrowers with seasonal short-term needs for capital.

A secured loan, on the other hand, requires a pledge of all or some of the assets of the business, to protect the lender against the risk of default. A secured loan gives the lender first claim over other creditors in collecting on its debt should the borrower default.

There are various types of secured loans. A liquid asset loan is secured by savings accounts, life insurance policies, and similar assets. In the case of the savings account, the account is restricted as to permissible transactions. In the case of the life insurance policy, you can either borrow directly against the policy's cash surrender value or you can use the cash surrender value as collateral for a loan. Other liquid assets such as stocks may also be used as collateral; however, because of market fluctuations, commercial lenders generally lend only up to 75 percent of the market value of even high-quality stocks.

Accounts receivable loans are those in which all or a portion of the company's accounts receivable are assigned as security for a loan. This can be accomplished either by directly assigning the money from accounts receivable to the lender, with the borrower still owing the receivables, or by factoring, in which the factor (the lender) buys outright the receivables, which are then no longer assets of the business. Factoring is relatively costly, since a factor generally levies a service charge of 1 or 2 percent on the face amount of the receivables purchased; this is separate and distinct from the interest charged for the period between the time the company receives the funds from the factor and the average maturity date of the receivables. Factoring helps a borrower who wishes to get out of the credit-collections function.

A number of other types of collateral are used to secure loans. In inventory financing, the bank does not take actual possession of the assets but appoints a third party (the warehouseman) to control the collateral to be released on the bank's instructions. Fast-moving inventory like clothing generally cannot be financed, but slower-moving items like automobiles may be.

In addition to asset-based loans, other forms of short-term financing are available. For example, depending on the kind of business, it may be possible to purchase goods on consignment, meaning that title remains with the consigner until the time of sale. Another possibility is a line of credit arrangement that allows the debtor to have a credit line, usually subject to annual renewal, with which to finance a specified percentage of the accounts receivable and inventory. A credit investigation precedes the extension of the line of credit, so that when the loan is actually needed, the funds are available.

29

SBA LOANS

Even with a mortgage on the corporate assets, many banks are reluctant to make loans to start-ups. However, often a bank will consider a lending program in conjunction with governmental agencies. This key describes the philosophy of and types of Small Business Administration (SBA) loans; more detailed information can be obtained by contacting the SBA directly or working through a loan packager. Although this key focuses on the standard SBA loans, special loans, such as those for veterans and for the handicapped, may also be available. In addition, other federal and state agencies, from the Economic Development Administration to state development companies, may provide small business financing.

The SBA was formed principally to aid, counsel, and protect small business in the United States. The SBA is not allowed to provide loans to those persons who can obtain financing from private sources; only if the loan is unobtainable elsewhere will the SBA consider providing funds on an immediate participation basis with a bank. The SBA also requires that there be a reasonable assurance of repayment and that the loan be for an appropriate business purpose. Further, the loan applicant must be of good character, demonstrate sufficient management expertise and commitment to run a business successfully, and have enough capital so that, with the loan, the business can be run prudently. Since new businesses must have enough capital to meet heavy start-up expenses and survive the initial operating period, the SBA generally requires new owners to invest a third to a half of the total assets needed to begin the business.

In the basic SBA guarantee loan, the SBA guarantees

as much as $350,000 or 90 percent, whichever is less, on loans made by private lenders. The maximum guarantee percentage of a loan exceeding $155,000 is 85 percent, but the SBA will guarantee up to $750,000 of a private-sector loan in certain cases.

A participation loan is a category of guarantee loans in which the lender and the SBA each provide part of the funds. The lender is responsible for collecting the payment and forwarding the appropriate amount to the SBA.

The SBA also makes direct loans, subject to a maximum of $150,000. The loans are available only to those individuals unable to obtain an SBA-guaranteed loan. This means that an applicant must first have applied to a commercial lender (those residing in larger cities must have applied to two lenders) and been rejected. Once the bank rejects the application, you need to get a decline letter stating the amount and term requested and the reason for the denial.

The process of applying for an SBA loan is straight-forward; your bank should be able to assist you. First, you must prepare a balance sheet; start-ups need to prepare an estimated balance sheet as of the date of opening. Second, you must submit income statements for the current period and for the three prior years, if available (start-ups should prepare a projection of earnings and expenses for at least the first year, with a monthly cash flow advisable). Third, you must prepare a current personal financial statement for each person who has an ownership interest in the business. Fourth, you must list the collateral being offered as security for the loan, along with an estimate of the current fair market value of each item. (The SBA requires that to the extent available, sufficient assets be pledged to secure the loan; it also requires personal guarantees from all of the principal owners as well as from the CEO. Moreover, liens on personal assets may be requested if the business assets are considered inadequate to secure a loan.) Next, you must state the amount of the loan requested and the purpose of the loan and take the material to a lender, who may charge a packaging fee to process the loan. Generally, this fee is refunded if the loan is denied.

If you are denied an SBA loan, you should write or visit the nearest SBA office on the chance that an error has been made. Strictly speaking, to qualify as a small business, the business must be operated for profit and, except for certain sheltered workshops, meet the SBA's "size" requirement; the SBA's definition of a small business is one that is independently owned and operated, that is not dominant in its field, and that meets certain minimal SBA standards for annual receipts, net worth, assets and/or the average number of employees. Thus, an agricultural business may be eligible for loans if yearly receipts are not over $1 million, while service businesses may qualify if annual receipts/sales do not exceed $3 million to $13.5 million.

If you obtain an SBA-guaranteed loan, the bank not only has an additional guarantee of payment (beyond any personal guarantees or security that you may have provided), but stands to make a profit by selling the guaranteed portion of the loan, thereby getting back most of its principal immediately and collecting a fee for its efforts. Since the bank's fee is geared to the size of the loan, banks are more interested in processing requests for larger loans than for smaller loans; the amount of work is nearly the same but the return is larger.

Before leaving the subject of SBA loans, it is worth noting that the SBA accepts businesses located in distressed areas, unlike most commercial lenders, allows a longer payback period than the three to five years banks want, and doesn't require as strong a credit rating. There are certain limitations, however. Some businesses, such as those involved in the dissemination of ideas, are ineligible for SBA loans; down payments are usually larger than those for regular loans; and the delay sometimes associated with getting an SBA loan may cause you to lose a deal, since the seller may not be willing to wait that long.

30

SELLER FINANCING

From the buyer's standpoint, seller financing can be a good deal. Sellers are not professional lenders and are not out to profit on the loan itself; therefore, interest rates tend to be lower, payback periods tend to be longer, and generally no points or other charges are imposed. Sellers will often lend a higher percentage of the purchase price than a commercial lender and might not foreclose the first time you miss a payment. Seller financing is inherently creative financing, and everything can be negotiated; the seller wants you to succeed and not to get in over your head. Further, you have an effective means of recourse that provides real leverage in the event a contractual breach is discovered.

Sellers of course prefer cash. The seller wants to get out of the business entirely without having to worry about getting paid. If you should default, the seller will have to sue to get the business back and try to resell it or a time when it may have been badly run down. The seller may want the money to retire, to go into another business, or for some other purpose. As a practical matter then, the seller accepts a tradeoff. It may be possible to find an all-cash buyer but only by accepting a substantially lower price. On the other hand, by carrying paper, the seller may be able to realize a substantially higher sales price.

Sellers can protect themselves by insisting on a shorter payback period, although the higher monthly payments may themselves trigger a bankruptcy. Of course, if a buyer defaults on an unsecured note, the seller can sue. But it is one thing to obtain a judgment and quite another to collect on that judgment. It is far better to have a security interest in the assets of the debtor, and what better assets than the assets being conveyed? Sellers can obtain additional protection by having the debtor pledge some personal assets, sign a personal guarantee, and perhaps provide a cosigner for the note. Such guarantees need not be unlimited; a guarantor might agree to be responsible for the first $10,000 of a $25,000 debt. Never sign a personal guarantee without your attorney's advice.

At a minimum, the seller should ensure that enough business assets are pledged to offer protection and that the security is adequately reflected in the purchase agreement, promissory note, security agreement, financing statement and guarantee. If selling stock, the seller should insist that the shares of stock be pledged as security.

The next step is to record either the security agreement or financing statement to place third parties on notice that it exists. For a financing statement, the standard form, the UCC-1, has space for the names and addresses of the debtor(s), the lender, secured party and the collateral being covered. Generally, the preparer of the financing statement lists the items of collateral in an addendum, although the level of detail will not be as great as that in a security agreement. When the note is satisfied, the creditor should complete a release of the financing statement as well as Form UCC-3 to document that action with the same filing officer(s) who recorded the initial financing statement. (The Form UCC-3 can also be used to amend the UCC-1).

In the case of a stock pledge, the seller takes a security interest in the stock being sold. The selling corporation is not a party to the pledge; it involves just the selling shareholders of the corporation and the buyer. If the stock pledge is drafted properly, the seller may, in the event of a default, sell all or any part of the security immediately, with or without notice, either at a public or private sale. Unfortunately, the shares of closely-held corporations have fairly limited marketability, especially since by the time of default, the business is likely to be in dire straits.

31

BUYING AND SELLING A BUSINESS: INTRODUCTION TO TAX ASPECTS

This key and the nine that follow consider the tax aspects of buying and selling a small business. This key presents an overview of the issues; succeeding keys cover more specialized topics.

Although some of the issues covered apply to corporate and noncorporate entities alike, this book emphasizes the purchase and sale of incorporated businesses. It also assumes that the purchaser wishes to operate the business in the corporate form and therefore will need to incorporate before signing the purchase agreement so that the corporation will be the purchaser; alternatively, the purchaser will sign the purchase agreement individually and then assign that contract to a newly-formed corporation.

The material that follows assumes some knowledge of taxation generally and corporate taxation in particular. Those needing a basic understanding of corporate tax matters might wish to read through the "Questions and Answers" section appearing at the end of this book before proceeding.

Initially, you need to consider whether to structure the business transfer as nontaxable or taxable. The nontaxable business transfer results from a reorganization under Section 368 of the Internal Revenue Code (see Key 32).

Taxable transfers are of two types: a sale of shares of stock and a sale of business assets.

For the seller, a stock sale is a simple transaction to effect and results in a capital gain, while the proceeds of the asset sale are ordinary income. For the buyer, however, an asset purchase is preferable since it avoids the unwitting assumption of hidden liabilities and allows the buyer to allocate the sales price to the various assets and to take a "step-up" or increase in tax basis of the assets purchased.

Simply put, all that "step-up" means is that the buyer increases the basis in the asset being acquired to its fair market value (FMV). For example, equipment with an FMV and an original basis of $10,000 might have been depreciated by the seller down to $5,000. In the case of a purchase of stock, the buyer would take a carryover basis of $5,000. In the case of a purchase of assets, however, the buyer can begin with a basis of $10,000 (subject to the allocation rules as set forth elsewhere). The buyer thus "steps up" the basis to the purchase price.

Thus, in an asset purchase, the buyer receives an immediate step-up in tax basis in the asset to the purchase price of the business, while in a stock purchase, the buyer receives a tax basis in the stock being acquired equal to the purchase price, helpful only when the stock is ultimately sold, and unless a Section 338 election (discussed below) is made, receives only a carryover basis in the assets obtained. Even Section 338 is not an efficient way to overcome this inherent disadvantage of a stock sale, since all of the built-in gain in the selling company's assets will be taxable to the corporation, and the benefits of any upward adjustments in the bases of depreciable assets or inventory will be recognized only over time. Therefore, a Section 338 election is likely to be advantageous only when the seller has loss or credit carryovers that can be utilized. The general rule is that when the FMV of the assets being sold exceeds their tax bases, an asset purchase is advisable; if the tax bases of the assets exceed their FMVs, a stock purchase is preferable.

From the standpoint of the corporate seller, the subsequent liquidation of the corporation following an asset sale results in the corporation paying tax on the excess of the FMVs of the various corporate assets over their respective tax bases and the corporate shareholders paying tax on the difference between the proceeds paid to them and their tax bases in the stock. Of course, if the corporation is not liquidated following the sale of the assets and the corporate "shell" is kept alive, this second tax will be avoided. However, the personal holding company tax may apply to such inactive companies, so caution is warranted.

Specifically, under Section 541, personal holding companies are subject to an additional tax of 28 percent on undistributed personal holding company income. This tax can be avoided if the corporation distributes as dividends all of its after-tax income or if the corporation invests substantially in real estate or in tax-free bonds or stock where the interest can accumulate without being subject to the tax; even so, the corporation may be subject to the accumulated earnings tax under Section 531. Still, keeping the company alive is worth considering for those shareholders who have a low tax basis in their shares and wish to avoid the large tax that would occur if they immediately liquidated the company. In any event, in the case of a sale of shares outright, the seller of those stocks, whether corporate or noncorporate, pays only a single tax on the difference between the proceeds received for the shares and the tax bases of the shares. Further, in general, the sale of stock results in a capital gain or loss to the seller, which is problematic in view of the limitations applicable to capital losses. Fortunately, under Section 1244, a loss on the sale of Section 1244 stock is treated as an ordinary, rather than as a capital, loss. For Section 1244 purposes, the initial capital invested in the company cannot exceed $1 million and the corporation must have derived more than 50 percent of its aggregate gross receipts for the past five years from sources other than investment activities. Although the tax attributes of the acquired corporation generally carry over in a stock purchase, Section 382 provides an exception to this rule. Under this section, if there has been an ownership change, the income that can be offset by net operating loss (NOL) carryovers is limited to the value of the loss corporation immediately before the change, multiplied by the long-term tax-exempt rate. The net operating loss is available only if the acquired corporation continues in the same business for at least two years; if it does not, the carryover is lost.

The procedures differ somewhat for a taxable acquisition of assets and of stock. In a taxable asset acquisition, the buyer needs to obtain appraisals of the seller's assets pursuant to Section 1060 in order to allocate the purchase price, and the asset sale must be reported to the IRS on Form 8594. (Although a complex topic, Section 1060 in essence requires that whenever a trade or business is sold in a taxable transaction, both buyer and seller must allocate the purchase price to each asset under the residual method; that is, by allocating the purchase price to assets in a specified order beginning with cash and ending with goodwill and going concern value.) The seller's board of directors hold a meeting to authorize the sale of assets, and the buyer or the buyer's board meets to authorize the purchase. The agreement is then executed, subject to approval by the selling company's shareholders. Subject to state law, those who disagree with the proposed transaction (called the dissenters) may be given appraisal rights that require the valuation of their shares. (Under the Revised Model Business Corporation Act, a shareholder is entitled to dissent from, and obtain payment of, the fair value of his or her shares in the event of certain mergers, share exchanges, amendments to the corporate articles, or the sale or exchange of all, or substantially all, of the corporate property other than in the usual and regular course of business if the shareholder is entitled to vote on the sale or exchange.)

Assuming that the parties do agree to the terms of the asset transfer, a bill of sale will be executed at the closing in exchange for the purchase price. If the selling corporation is liquidated, it will distribute its assets to the shareholders in exchange for the shareholders' stock, which is then cancelled. The corporation must then notify the IRS within 30 days after approval of the liquidation by filing Form 966, as well as satisfy any state law requirements respecting liquidation and provide tax information for its final corporate tax return in accordance with IRS regulations.

In the case of a taxable acquisition of stock, the buyers deal directly with the shareholders. After the buyer or the buyer's board has approved the purchase, a stock purchase agreement is executed. As noted earlier, the actual endorsement of the shares and issuance of new shares is relatively simple; the tax problem with a stock sale is that the buyer retains a carryover basis in the assets acquired, which generally translates to a lower basis than would be the case with an asset purchase. To avoid this, a deemed asset sale under Section 338, which does allow a step-up in tax basis in the seller's assets, might be considered. Section 338, which applies only to corporate purchasers, provides that, if the stock of a corporation (target) is acquired by such a buyer in a qualified stock purchase, the purchasing corporation may elect to treat the seller as if it had sold, in a single transaction, all of its assets (as old target) and then purchased those assets (as new target). The new target is deemed to have purchased those assets at the beginning of the day following the acquisition date. Put somewhat differently, if an election under Section 338 is made, the purchased corporation is treated as if it had sold all of its assets at their FMV, so the purchaser may obtain the FMV basis in assets even if the transaction is a stock purchase.

If Section 338 is elected, it is necessary to obtain appraisals. As noted earlier, there are problems with Section 338, so the Section 338 (h)(10) election should be considered, in which case the buyer will get a step-up in tax basis of the assets but face fewer tax problems. In any event, at the closing, the stock of the shareholders will be exchanged for cash or other property. If the purchasing corporation decides to liquidate the new subsidiary, the seller's board must approve this and obtain any necessary shareholder approvals. Again, Form 966 must be filed with the IRS, state law requirements must be satisfied, and the information on the final corporate tax return must be provided. Special rules apply in the case of the liquidation of S corporations.

32

REORGANIZATIONS

Under the Internal Revenue Code (IRC), seven types of reorganizations qualify as nontaxable exchanges. The theory here is that if a taxpayer has simply converted an investment in one corporation to an investment in another corporation, no taxable event is deemed to have occurred, and any gain or loss will ultimately be recognized upon liquidation of the investment. Thus, a reorganization results in a carryover basis in the nonrecognition property received (i.e., the nonrecognition property takes the same basis as the property exchanged.)

Regardless of the form of reorganization, the stock or securities received must be the stock or securities of a party to the reorganization. (Parties to the reorganization include either the acquired and acquiring corporation, if the stock or securities of the parent is used, and any new corporation formed in the course of the reorganization). The plan of reorganization must satisfy certain requirements and there must be a bona fide business purpose for the transaction, which means it cannot be done just to realize tax savings. In addition, there must be a continuity of the shareholder's interest through membership in the acquiring corporation; continuity of the business enterprise is also required. Should a reorganization fail to meet the strict requirements of the statute, the IRS will deny it tax-free status.

The first of the seven types of reorganization that qualify for tax-free treatment is the Type A reorganization. A Section 368(a)(1)(A) reorganization entails a statutory merger or consolidation (a merger is a union of two or more corporations in which one of the corporations retains its corporate existence and absorbs the other; a consolidation is the formation of a new corporation to take the place of two or more constituent corporations that subsequently lose their corporate existence).

The second type is the Type B reorganization. A Section 368(a)(1)(B) reorganization entails the acquisition by one corporation, in exchange solely for all or part of its voting stock, of stock of another corporation, if immediately after the acquisition, the acquiring corporation has control of the other corporation. Control for this purpose means at least 80 percent of the total combined voting power and at least 80 percent of the total number of shares of all other classes of stock. As an example, if X corporation exchanges its voting stock for the required statutory control of Y corporation, this qualifies as a Type B reorganization and Y will become a subsidiary of X. A Type B reorganization is relatively easy to accomplish if the target is closely held but more difficult to effect if the shares are widely held. Since the corporation continues to exist, shareholder meetings are unnecessary and the dissenting shareholders generally have no appraisal rights.

The third type is the Type C reorganization. In a Section 368 (a)(1)(C) reorganization, the acquiring corporation must obtain substantially all the assets of the target corporation in exchange for the voting stock of the acquiring corporation. For example, if X corporation acquires substantially all of the assets of Y corporation by transferring common stock of X corporation, that qualifies as a Type C reorganization. The acquiring corporation in a Type C reorganization assumes only those liabilities it wishes to assume and is not liable for unknown or contingent claims as long as it has met the state's bulk sales act requirements. A recurring problem in this area is defining what constitutes "substantially all" of the assets. Generally, the buyer needs to acquire at least 90 percent of the FMV of the net assets of the seller and at least 70 percent of the FMV of the gross assets. Although the IRS, to date, has not set exact rules, the foregoing tests generally bring a reorganization within the "safe harbor." It should be noted that the value of the cash or other property received in addition to the stock of the purchasing corporation may not be in excess of 20 percent of the total value received in the transaction, since 80 percent of the assets must be obtained for the voting stock.

The fourth type is the Type D (divisive) reorganization. In a Section 368(a)(1)(D) reorganization, a parent corporation transfers some or all of the assets of one corporation to another corporation.

There are three types of divisive reorganizations:

1. The spin-off, in which a corporation transfers a part of its business assets to a corporation that it controls and then distributes all of the controlled corporation's stock to its own shareholders.
2. The split-up, in which a corporation transfers all of its business assets to two or more newly-formed corporations in exchange for their stock, which the first corporation distributes to its shareholders in exchange for all of its own stock.
3. The split-off, in which a corporation transfers part of its business assets to a newly-formed corporation in exchange for the new corporation's stock, which it then distributes to its own shareholders in exchange for a part of its own stock.

Even though obtaining a private letter ruling from the IRS is not a requirement for tax-free reorganization treatment, as a practical matter, a corporate division is usually done only after obtaining such a ruling. To do otherwise may cause the IRS auditor to challenge the validity of the reorganization at a later date.

The fifth type is the Type E reorganization. A Section 368(a)(1)(E) reorganization does not involve an acquisitive or divisive reorganization but is merely an alteration of the corporation's debt or equity; for example, substituting preferred stock that was previously authorized but unissued for outstanding common stock.

The sixth type is the Type F reorganization. A Section 368 (a)(1)(F) reorganization entails a mere change in the identity, form or place or organization of one corporation. Thus, if a corporation merely changes its name, this is not considered a taxable event.

The seventh type is the Type G reorganization. A Section 368(a)(1)(G) reorganization involves the distribution of all or some portion of the assets of a corporation to another corporation as part of a reorganization in bankruptcy. The shareholders of the corporation distributing the assets must have a continuing interest in the distributee corporation and must receive stock in the transaction.

In sum, the general rules of recognition of gain or loss on exchanges do not apply to certain exchanges that relate to mere changes in corporate structure and hence cause only an adjustment of the continuing interests in property, with no gain or loss to be recognized by either the corporation or the shareholders. The advice of an attorney whose practice emphasizes the tax aspects of a reorganization is advised if you venture into this area.

33

SECTION 1060:
PART 1

Most small acquisitions are taxable-asset purchases subject to the strictures of Section 1060, the subject of this Key, and the three that follow.

By way of background, the sale of all the assets of a business for a lump sum is considered by the IRS to be a sale of each asset and not the sale of a single capital asset. The buyer must allocate the total sales price paid among the assets acquired to determine the basis of the asset acquired. The seller, in turn, must allocate the sales price to determine the amount realized on the sale of each asset.

Prior to the adoption of the Tax Reform Act of 1986, the seller and buyer had opposite interests regarding the allocation of the sales price to an asset sale. The seller wanted to allocate as much of the sales price as possible to nonamortizable assets like goodwill or going concern value in order to benefit from the capital gains deduction and to use the installment method for reporting taxable gain. The seller wanted to avoid allocation of the sales price to the depreciable and amortizable assets, because such an allocation would trigger depreciation recapture and the gain would be treated as ordinary income. The buyer, meanwhile wished to allocate as much of the sales price as possible to the depreciable and amortizable assets to maximize later deductions; since no tax deduction was permitted for that part of the sales price allocated to nondepreciable, nonamortizable assets like goodwill, the buyer would have to wait until the business was sold again to realize any tax benefit.

Given the conflicting interests between buyer and

seller, the IRS tended to respect contractual allocations unless they were clearly unreasonable or there was in reality no adverse relationship. This all changed with the enactment of the Tax Reform Act of 1986 which repealed the capital gains deduction; consequently, no tax differential now exists between capital gains and ordinary income.

Since capital gains are now taxed on the same basis as ordinary income, for the most part, a seller is no longer concerned with sales price allocation, because there is no advantage for the seller in placing a higher value on goodwill unless perhaps the seller has large capital losses to utilize. Congress understandably became concerned that the tax interests of buyer and seller would no longer be adverse. Faced with the possibility that the seller might be able to extract a higher sales price from the buyer in exchange for agreeing to the buyer's allocation desires, it enacted Section 1060, which applies both to the buyer's tax basis in the assets and to the seller's gain or loss on the sale of those assets. Section 1060 applies to actual asset sales; the key on Section 338 considers so-called "deemed asset" sales. (See Key 38.)

Section 1060 provides that the "residual" method of allocation must be used to allocate the sales price in any applicable asset acquisition defined as any transfer, direct or indirect, of assets that constitutes a trade or business in the hands of the transferee determined wholly by the amount of consideration paid for such assets. Thus, Section 1060 applies not just to the sale of assets of corporations but to the sale of assets of unincorporated businesses, partnership interests, etc. According to the IRS regulations implementing Section 1060, a group of assets constituting a trade or business in either the hands of the buyer or the seller constitutes a trade or business for this purpose.

As noted, under the new law, both parties to an applicable asset acquisition must use the residual method. Under this method, the sales price for the assets being transferred is allocated sequentially according to the as-

118

sets' respective FMVs based on which of four classes of assets they are in. The four classes of assets are:

- **Class I assets:** cash, demand deposits, and similar accounts up to their FMVs in banks, savings and loan institutions, and other depository institutions
- **Class II assets:** certificates of deposit, U.S. Government securities, readily marketable stock or securities, and foreign currency in proportion to their respective FMVs on the purchase date
- **Class III assets:** all other transferred assets not included in Class I or Class II in proportion to their FMVs on the purchase date.
- **Class IV assets:** intangible assets, either goodwill or going concern value

As noted, goodwill and going concern value are identified as Class IV assets. For this purpose, goodwill is the value inherent in the favorable patronage of a business by customers arising from the fact that it is an established and well-known enterprise; the IRS has ruled that the presence of goodwill is evidenced by the potential of a business to generate a return in excess of the industry average on tangible assets. Going concern value on the other hand, is the enhanced asset value inherent in a business already in operation. Going concern value includes the capacity of a business to generate a return without interruption despite a change in ownership. One way to look at going concern value is to calculate what would have been a fair return or loss on your investment during the nonproductive start-up period that was avoided by your purchase of a going concern.

Since goodwill and going concern value do not have a limited life that can be estimated with any degree of reasonable accuracy, goodwill and going concern value are not amortizable capital assets with a current tax benefit. Under the residual method imposed by Section 1060, assets not falling in Class I, Class II, or Class III, are automatically forced into this category. Although there is at present no distinction between goodwill and going concern value, there is still a good reason for separating the Class IV intangibles from intangibles such as covenants not to compete, that are amortizable. This is a difficult task that requires you to demonstrate that the amortizable intangible has a limited life that can be estimated with reasonable accuracy and is susceptible to a separate valuation. (See Key 35.)

34

SECTION 1060:
PART 2

This key provides a detailed example of the workings of Section 1060. Assume a corporation is owned by a single shareholder with a tax basis in his or her shares of $100. The shareholder receives an offer of $3100 for the gross assets of the business based on their FMVs. Alternatively, the prospective buyer offers $2100 for either the stock or the net assets of the corporation, based on the FMV of the shareholders' equity section of the balance sheet.

An examination of the corporate balance sheet discloses just four assets: cash, with a tax basis of $100 and an FMV of the same; accounts receivable, with a tax basis of $300 and an FMV of $300; inventory, with a tax basis of $500 and an FMV of $700; and equipment, with a tax basis of $600 and an FMV of $1000.

The balance sheet discloses current liabilities with a tax basis and an FMV of $300 and a mortgage with a tax basis and an FMV of $700. The capital is shown at $100 and the retained earnings at $400. This means that the total assets of $1500 equals the total liabilities and shareholders' equity of $1500.

Since the FMV of the corporate liabilities is $1000 and the FMV of the shareholders' equity is ostensibly $2100 based on the offer of this amount the FMV of the liabilities and shareholders' equity combined must be $3100. Therefore, the FMV of the total assets must also be $3100. Since the FMV of the specifically identifiable assets is only $2100, the difference of $1000 must be goodwill.

Assume that a sale of stock for the $2100 is agreed to be the parties. To determine the tax effect on the shareholder, subtract the sales price ($2100) from the shareholder's basis in the shares ($100) to arrive at a gain of $2000. Assuming a tax rate of 28 percent at the shareholder level, the tax due is $560; the net proceeds to the shareholder would be $2100 minus $560, or $1540. The foregoing does not consider the effect of installment reporting, the alternative minimum tax, any other capital gains or losses the shareholder might have, or any other issues affecting the shareholder's particular tax situation. Section 1060 has not been mentioned yet because it concerns only applicable asset acquisitions.

Now, assume the buyer wants to buy the gross assets of the business, without assuming its liabilities, for $3100. To determine the tax effect, you must divide the assets into the various classes, determine the gain or loss on an asset-by-asset basis, and then allocate the sales price to the classes to the extent of, but not in excess of, their FMVs.

Cash is a Class I asset with a tax basis and an FMV of $100. There is no gain to be recognized here, and none of the sales price needs to be allocated here either. The accounts receivable is a Class III asset with a tax basis and an FMV of $300; no gain need be recognized here either. The inventory is a Class III asset but here the $200 difference between the tax basis of $500 and the FMV of $700 is considered to be ordinary income to the seller. The equipment is also a Class III asset; here the difference between the tax basis of $600 and the FMV of $1000 is $400, which is also ordinary income.

Total ordinary income comes to $600. There is a Class IV asset (goodwill), however, that has an FMV of $1000. Since the tax basis of the goodwill is $0, there must be a capital gain arising out of the transfer of that goodwill of $1000. Thus, if the corporation sells the assets for $3100, without the buyer assuming any liabilities, it must record a capital gain of $1000 and ordinary income of $600. Since ordinary income and capital gains are now both taxed at the same rate, if you assume an applicable corporate tax rate of 34 percent, the tax on the total income of $1600 comes to $544 for the seller.

Had stock been sold instead of the assets, the gain ($2100 selling price minus $100 tax basis) of $2000 would have resulted in a tax of $560 to the selling shareholder. In one case, the seller is the corporation itself; in the other case, the seller is the individual shareholder.

If the seller wants to liquidate the corporation through a plan of complete liquidation and distribute the assets to the shareholder who will in turn transfer the assets to the buyer, the corporation must recognize income on the distribution of assets as if the assets had been sold at their FMVs; that is, there will be a corporate level tax on any net gain in addition to the tax imposed at the shareholder level. In this case, the shareholder must treat the receipt of the net assets as full payment in exchange for the stock and realize a capital gain as follows: subtract from the FMV of the assets ($3100) both the tax liability arising from the corporate distribution ($544) and the other liabilities assumed in the transaction ($1000), leaving a net amount of $1556. Next, subtract the shareholder's tax basis in the shares ($100) to arrive at the shareholder's capital gain of $1456. The tax to the shareholder, assuming a 28 percent marginal tax rate, is therefore $408.

This example considers only the federal tax impact of the proposed business transfer; there may be other tax implications as well. Generally, the sale of business assets that are tangible personal property used in the conduct of an active trade or business is subject to sales tax unless exempt. (Certain categories of property, such as inventory, are generally purchased for resale and are exempt; in addition, most states provide that an occasional sale exempts a transaction from tax.) Of course, the foregoing discussion relates only to transfers of assets—a stock sale does not involve the transfer of tangible personal property and thus there will generally be no sales tax imposed. However, certain states such as Florida do impose a documentary stamp tax on such transfers.

35

SECTION 1060:
PART 3

Because Class IV offers no tax benefits; buyers try to find other intangible assets—the Class III intangibles—that can be separated from goodwill and going concern value and thus provide a direct tax benefit.

For an intangible to qualify as a Class III asset, it must have a limited useful life that can be estimated with reasonable accuracy. According to the IRS, "If an intangible asset is known from experience or other facts to be of use in the business or in the production of income for only a limited period, the length of which can be estimated with reasonable accuracy, such an intangible asset may be the subject of a depreciation allowance. Examples are patents and copyrights. An intangible asset, the useful life of which is not limited, in not subject to an allowance for depreciation." The challenge, therefore, is to separate by identity and value such amortizable intangibles from the nonamortizable goodwill and going-concern value.

In addition to patents and copyrights, amortizable intangibles include, for example, covenants not to compete, customer lists, and favorable leases and contracts. The covenant not to compete, which is especially difficult to establish as a Class III asset, is considered here in some depth.

A covenant not to compete generally prohibits a seller of a business from engaging in the same business as the buyer for a specified period of time and over a specified geographic area. In the absence of a statute to the contrary, the courts enforce covenants not to compete to the extent reasonably necessary to protect the buyer's investment in the goodwill of the business; to do otherwise would enable the seller to ruin the very business he or she had just sold.

The legal theory here is that the purchaser of a business buys more than just the tangible assets of the business, since goodwill also passes in the transaction. The courts have repeatedly held that the sale of a business is sufficient consideration for a covenant not to compete and have inferred the sale of goodwill from the mere presence of a covenant not to compete. Conversely, some courts have inferred a covenant not to compete from the sale of goodwill, but such findings tend to be more limited than if there is an express covenant not to compete.

Covenants not to compete are treated differently from goodwill for tax purposes. Whereas goodwill is not amortizable, covenants not to compete are taxed in the same fashion as compensation for agreeing to perform services; that is, it is taxable as ordinary income to the recipient/seller. For the buyer, the amount allocated to the covenant not to compete represents a purchased intangible, amortizable over the term of the agreement.

Thus, it is in the buyer's interest from a tax standpoint to establish that a covenant not to compete exists as an asset separate from the goodwill. Two tests have been used for this purpose: the economic reality test and the specific allocation test.

Under the economic reality test, a seller must represent a viable competitive threat to the buyer; if the former owner doesn't represent a real competitive threat to the new owner in the absence of a covenant not to compete, then such a covenant will not be respected for tax purposes. Various factors, such as the seller's advanced age, poor health, or entry into an unrelated business following closing, tend to diminish the likelihood—the economic reality—of such a threat.

Under the specific allocation test, also known as the severability test, the courts have focused on the severability of a covenant not to compete from goodwill—that is, whether the covenant was negotiated separately from the underlying agreement. Any consideration received for a covenant not to compete should therefore be specifically allocated and be given separately. Not only should the covenant not to compete be placed in a separate contract, but an agreement calling for the sellers to stay on in the post-closing period should be placed in a separate contract as well.

Since a lump sum payment by the buyer to the seller looks more like goodwill than payment for a covenant not to compete, the preferred approach is to avoid such one-shot payments. Some planners suggest combining the covenant with a consulting agreement, since such an agreement has basically the same tax consequences for buyer and seller but reduces the likelihood of an IRS challenge. For the seller, both forms of payment are recognized as ordinary income; for the buyer, payments under the covenant not to compete are amortized over the life of the covenant whereas payments under a consulting agreement are deductible as incurred. Allotting a part of the covenant not to compete to the consulting agreement may help in the face of an audit challenge. In either event, the buyer should clearly document the value of the covenant. Professional valuation services can be of assistance in valuing the purchased intangibles as well as in determining their useful lives, and the IRS is more likely to respect the judgment of an independent valuator's findings than those developed by persons with an interest in the outcome.

36

SECTION 1060:
PART 4

This key considers federal income tax reporting requirements under Section 1060. The IRS has promulgated regulations implementing the section that require the seller and buyer each to file as part of their federal tax returns for the year Form 8594 which contains certain information about the allocation of consideration among the assets being transferred.

Information included on Form 8594 includes the name, address, and taxpayer identifying number (TIN) of the buyer and seller (buyer and seller thus need to exchange TINs), the date of the sale, the total sales price (i.e., the consideration paid for the assets), the amount of consideration allocable to each class of assets, and the aggregate FMV of the assets of each class, a statement as to whether the buyer and seller provided for an allocation of the sales price in the sales agreement or in another document, the useful life of each Class III intangible and amortizable asset, and a statement as to whether the buyer also obtained a license or covenant not to compete or entered into a lease agreement, employment contract, management contract, or similar agreement with the seller.

It should be clear from this description that the total sales price includes not just the cash and other property given to the seller but also the amount of any liabilities. The form does not require a signed, written agreement between the parties detailing the allocation of consideration of the aggregate FMV of each of the four asset classes, although it is considered good practice to have one.

The law does require that a supplemental Form 8594

127

be filed with the federal tax return of each party to the transaction for any taxable year in which there is an adjustment to the amount of the consideration. Generally, increases in consideration are allocated among the assets transferred under the general allocation rules, while decreases in consideration are allocated first among goodwill/going concern value and then among the other assets in their order of class, first to Class III, then to Class II, and finally to Class I. Special rules apply for allocating changes in consideration for certain intangibles, such as patents.

For example, assume that T corporation sells a group of assets constituting a trade or business to M corporation. For simplicity, assume that there are only two specifically identifiable assets: marketable securities worth $200 (a Class II asset) and equipment valued at $1000 (a Class III asset), for a total FMV of $1200. Now, assume there are liabilities in the amount of $400. M corporation offers $600 cash for the assets and intends to assume the liabilities of $400.

To allocate the $1000 of consideration paid pursuant to Section 1060, first allocate to Class I. In this case, there is no entry. Then allocate to Class II. The amount allocable to Class II is $200, reducing the purchase price to $800. The amount allocable to Class III is $1000, leaving $200 of excess consideration to go to Class IV goodwill/going concern value.

Two years after filing Form 8594 the buyer settles a lawsuit against the seller alleging fraud in the sale. The buyer receives $250 in the settlement. How is this sum to be reported? A reallocation is necessary. The $250 received from the seller reduces the total consideration paid by the buyer by that amount. Of that reduction, $200 is allocated to Class IV, reducing goodwill to $0. The remainder of $50 is used to reduce the Class III asset from $1000 to $950. If there is more than one asset in any class, the procedure is to allocate the decrease in consideration among the various assets based on their FMVs as of the acquisition date.

Filing Form 8594 is an important step in any asset acquisition. The failure to file this form or to include correct information may result in penalties. Therefore, even if you have some doubt as to its applicability, it might be a good idea to file the form in any situation where Section 1060 could apply.

37

CORPORATE LIQUIDATIONS

The liquidation of the corporate shell is a central step in many sales of small businesses. The corporation may sell its assets and then liquidate or it may liquidate first and then distribute its assets to the shareholders, who in turn dispose of them. A complete liquidation results when the corporation distributes all of the assets in exchange for all of the outstanding stock.

The tax results to the shareholders are these: a distribution made in complete liquidation is treated as a full payment for the shareholder's stock, with the shareholder reporting gain or loss measured by the difference between the value of the assets received in the liquidating distribution and the basis for the stock surrendered.

Prior to the passage of the Tax Reform Act of 1986, a corporation was generally not taxed when it made such a liquidating distribution, which meant that the corporation did not report income when it distributed any appreciated asset, nor would it recognize a loss when it distributed an asset that had gone down in value. This was known as the *General Utilities* rule after a famous case by that name. The 1986 Act repealed this rule, however, and a corporation must now report gain or loss on the distribution of assets other than cash in complete liquidation; the corporation is treated as if it had sold the assets at their FMVs to the shareholders.

If an asset is subject to a liability, or if the shareholders assume the liability, and the liability exceeds the asset's FMV, its value is deemed to be the amount of the liability and the corporation recognizes gain to the extent that the liability exceeds the asset's basis. In like manner, a sale of assets in the course of a complete liquidation is generally taxable; the corporate seller recognizes gain or loss when it sells the assets and the shareholder pays a second tax on the net proceeds of a liquidating distribution.

There are two important issues here concerning valuation and installment reporting of gains. The burden of establishing the FMV of an asset rests generally with the distributing corporation, which must file Form 1099-DIV with the IRS for each shareholder to whom a distribution is made. This form records the amount of money distributed, if any, listing separately each other class of property distributed in the liquidation, describes the property in each class, and states the FMV at the time of the distribution. For this purpose, the value of realty is usually obtained through independent professional appraisers; best estimates may be used for many other assets. When property is sold to an unrelated party shortly after the liquidation, the selling price normally establishes the FMV, based on the fundamental IRS principle of valuation that value refers to the "price at which the property would change hands between a willing buyer and willing seller, neither being under any compulsion to buy or sell and both having a reasonable knowledge of relevant facts."

If a corporation adopts a plan of complete liquidation and, on or after the date of the adoption of the plan, sells property in return for the buyer's notes and completely liquidates within twelve months after the date of the adoption of the plan, the shareholder may report the FMV of the notes on the installment method. For example, assume a corporation adopts a plan of liquidation and sells all of the assets to the buyer for $100,000, $25,000 in cash and the balance of $75,000, in five annual promissory notes of $15,000 each. The selling corporation has no liabilities and distributes the cash and notes to its sole shareholder within twelve months after adoption of the plan of liquidation. The shareholder's tax basis in the stock is $20,000. How much gain must be reported if the installment method is used?

First, the shareholder has a capital gain (long term, if

so qualified) of $20,000. To compute this, take the sales price of the stock ($25,000 plus $75,000, or $100,000); subtract the shareholder's tax basis in the shares of $20,000, leaving a gross profit to the shareholder of $80,000. The gross profit percentage is therefore 80 percent. To compute the capital gain, multiply the cash received ($25,000) by the gross profit percentage of 80 percent which yields a gain of $20,000. As the notes are collected in the succeeding years, the normal installment method rules apply.

Thus, the installment method allows a taxpayer to defer recognition of gain on seller-financed sales until income is actually realized.

A couple of examples may be helpful to illustrate the effects of a corporate liquidation in the context of a business transfer. Assume the owner of a corporation has decided to liquidate a company whose assets currently have an FMV of $200,000. The corporation has a tax basis in the assets of $100,000 and the shareholder's tax basis in the shares is $100,000.

If the corporation is liquidated, it will pay a corporate-level tax of $100,000, since the liquidation is treated as if the corporation had sold all of the assets for their FMVs (here, $200,000 minus $100,000). At a marginal tax rate of 34 percent, the tax due the IRS will be $34,000, leaving the corporation $166,000 in assets for distribution to the shareholders.

For the shareholder, a distribution in complete liquidation is treated as a full payment for the stock. The shareholder recognizes gain equal to the difference between the FMV of the assets received and the tax basis in the stock. Since the shareholder's basis in the stock is $100,000, the recognized gain must be $66,000 (i.e., the $166,000 of net proceeds distributed to the shareholder minus the $100,000 basis). This results in a $18,480 second tax to the shareholder (i.e., 28 percent of the $66,000 gain) leaving the shareholder $147,520 in after-tax assets. The tax adds up to $52,480, consisting of $34,000 in tax at the corporate level and $18,480 at the shareholder level. Since the gain was $100,000 the effective tax rate on the liquidation is 52.48 percent.

Prior to the repeal of the *General Utilities* rule, the tax rate on a liquidation was generally 20 percent, since the corporation could have been liquidated tax-free and the shareholders would have been subject only to a 20 percent capital gains tax on the receipt of the assets in liquidation. In the post-1986 Act era, the rate has been raised to 52.48 percent, assuming that the shareholder is an individual; for corporate shareholders, the effective tax rate is now 45.44 percent.

Now, consider a different example. Assume the shareholder of a corporation has been offered $25,000 for either the stock or the assets of a corporation. The corporation has a tax basis in the assets of $50,000, but the FMV of the assets is $25,000. The shareholder has a tax basis in the shares of $20,000.

If the shareholder sells the stock, he or she will recognize a gain equal to the difference between the basis in the shares ($10,000) and the sales price ($25,000), or $15,000. The gain is taxed once at a 28 percent tax rate.

Now, assume a sale of assets by the corporation, rather than a sale of stock. The corporation's gain or loss is calculated by subtracting the basis in the assets ($50,000) from the sales price ($25,000), for a $25,000 loss. If the corporation is liquidated immediately, no tax is imposed, but the shareholder pays a tax on the gain based on the difference between the cash received $25,000), and the basis in the shares ($10,000). Thus, the tax effect is the same. Note, however, that the $25,000 loss on the sale has been entirely lost and will evaporate upon the liquidation of the corporation.

What should the shareholder do? The answer depends on whether the assets are low basis or high basis and what the shareholder would like to do with the cash. A shareholder who does not intend to start another business should probably sell the stock. The buyer could then use the high basis in the corporate assets to reduce the gain if the assets appreciate in value or to take the loss when selling the assets. The tax effect is the same either way to the selling shareholder. However, a shareholder who wants to start another business should have the corporation sell assets, since the corporate shell could then be used (i.e., the corporate shell remaining after liquidation for tax purposes need not be dissolved under state law). The gain to the shareholder on the liquidation is deferred, and the selling shareholder may be able to use all or some of the loss on the asset sale to offset gain at a later time.

The foregoing provides some idea of the issues involved in liquidating a corporation; other factors can play a role as well. Be sure to work with your tax adviser in this area.

38

A LOOK AT SECTION 338

Most buyers of small businesses prefer to purchase assets over stock. Although the process of transferring title to the various assets can be time-consuming, at least the buyer is clear about what is being bought. From a tax standpoint, the buyer can, subject to the strictures of Section 1060, allocate the purchase price to the underlying assets of the target and then take a step-up in tax basis to the asset's FMV.

The corporate seller, however, may resist a sale of assets because such a sale is considered to be a taxable event, with gain or loss recognized by comparing the tax basis of the various assets to the sales price. In addition, the shareholders who receive distributions of the cash proceeds are subject to a second tax, regardless of whether the distribution takes the form of a dividend or a liquidation.

The buyer wants the step-up in tax basis that is possible with an asset sale, but the seller does not like the double tax resulting from such a sale. What about a sale of stock? A sale of stock by the owners is a one-step transaction that results in only a single tax on the shareholder's gain and lowers the tax rate from 52.48 percent to 28 percent for an individual shareholder and from 56.44 percent to 34 percent for a corporate shareholder.

Since the corporation is itself unchanged in a stock sale, such a transfer has no effect on the basis of the acquired corporation's assets. The goal thus becomes to find a way to structure a stock sale so the buyer can still take a step-up in the basis of the assets. Under Section 338, which is applicable only to corporate buyers, a corporation may elect to treat a stock purchase as an asset purchase. This is known as a "qualified purchase." Specifically, a corporation acquiring the stock of another corporation may elect to treat the purchase price of the stock as the purchase price of the assets of the corporation being acquired (i.e., the acquiring corporation obtains a basis in the target corporation's assets.)

To qualify for such special treatment, the acquiring corporation must have purchased, during a period of not more than 12 months, at least 80 percent of the voting stock and 80 percent of the total shares of all classes of stock other than nonvoting preferred.

In a Section 338 election, which must be made by the purchasing corporation within 75 days after it acquires the 80 percent control, the target corporation is treated as if it had undergone a complete liquidation, conveying all of its assets in one transaction at the close of the day on which the purchaser achieved the 80 percent control (the acquisition date). The target is treated as a new corporation that has bought all of the assets at the beginning of the day following the acquisition. This is known as a "deemed liquidation."

Prior to the enactment of the Tax Reform Act of 1986, a deemed liquidation could usually be structured so that neither gain nor loss would be recognized on the sale of the target's assets. That loophole has been closed, however, so that a Section 338 election results in a double tax. The basis of the assets deemed to have been purchased by new target depends on the purchaser's basis for the target's stock on the acquisition date. Assuming that the purchaser buys all of the target's stock, the entire basis of the shares is allocated to the target's assets.

Further, the old target must recognize income to the extent that the "deemed sales price" exceeds its basis in the assets. The buyer must pay the tax, and the new target, as the purchaser, is regarded as a corporation with no tax attributes, such as earnings and profits. In fact, a prime disadvantage of Section 338 is that any tax attributes of the old target not used in its final tax return are lost forever. Another disadvantage of Section 338 is that not only does the old target recognize income to the extent that the deemed sales price exceeds its adjusted basis in its assets, but the buyer cannot use its net operating losses to offset any gain which has to be recognized.

There is at least one case where a Section 338 election may be advisable: When the target's net operating loss approximately equals that of the gain anticipated by utilizing the election, thereby allowing a step-up in tax basis since the target is permitted to use its net operating losses to offset the gain from the Section 338 election. Note that any net operating losses that remain are lost.

Given the problems inherent in Section 338, however, buyers sometimes try to structure a stock deal as an asset deal allowing basis step-up for tax purposes. This may be possible under a Section 338(h)(10) election; in which a buyer and seller, under specified circumstances, jointly elect to treat a sale of stock as an asset sale taking place while the target is still a member of the seller's consolidated group. Following the sale, the target is treated as if it had been liquidated into the seller. In other words, the target is treated as if it had sold all of its assets to the buyer, although, in reality, the target's corporate parent has sold the target's stock to the buyer. The effect is that the seller is not taxed on the gain from the actual stock sale but from the deemed sale.

In sum, under Section 338(h)(10) the sale of the stock is treated as an asset sale to the buyer and the buyer receives a step-up in basis in the target's assets. The seller, meanwhile, is responsible for paying any tax due, recognizing gain not on the actual stock sale but on the deemed sale of assets, that is, the deemed sales price minus the tax basis in the assets. (In a Section 338 election, the buyer is responsible for any tax triggered on the deemed sale.) The target is permitted to use any net operating losses to offset any gain required to be recognized. Since the target is deemed liquidated into the seller, any unused tax attributes of the target pass to the seller. (In a Section 338 election, the tax attributes do not carry over but are wiped out.) Section 338(h)(10) is a complex provision; the decision on whether to use it depends on the availability of net operating losses, the presence of tax attributes, and similar factors. In the final analysis, the decision between Section 338 and Section 338(h)(10) depends on who is the one with the largest net operating loss and hence the one who is best able to minimize the overall tax liability from the transaction.

39

LIQUIDATION OF S CORPORATIONS

When an S corporation conveys assets, the share-holders of the corporation receive a pass-through of the gain equal to the increase in the basis in the stock. When the sales proceeds are actually distributed to the share-holders, the shareholders determine their gain or loss by comparing the value of the property received in the distribution to the adjusted basis in the stock; the basis increase allows the shareholders to receive tax-free distributions equal to the increase in basis. A stock sale has similar results, since the shareholders recognize gain by comparing the value of the cash received for the stock to the adjusted basis of the shares.

As noted previously, with the repeal of the *General Utilities rule*, regular (C) corporations are now required to recognize gain or loss on the distribution of their property in complete liquidation as if the property had been sold to the distributee at its FMV. However, the rules are different in the liquidation of an S corporation.

Prior to the passage of the Tax Reform Act of 1986, gain on appreciated property distributed by an S corporation in complete liquidation was not recognized at the corporate level; the shareholder recognized any gain measured by the FMV of the assets received minus the tax basis in the shareholder's stock.

Under the provisions of the Tax Reform Act of 1986, if an S corporation makes a distribution of property with respect to its stock and the FMV of the property exceeds the S corporation's basis in such assets, then gain is recognized by the S corporation as if it had sold the assets at their FMVs. Further, under new Section 1374, an S corporation is required to recognize corporate-level gain over a ten-year period, beginning with the first day of the first year for which the corporation is under S corporation status.

The reason for new Section 1374 is simple: since the new tax act provides for corporate recognition of gain on sales or distributions of property in the course of liquidation of a regular (C) corporation, such a company need only convert to S corporation status to avoid tax on the gain. The fact that under the Tax Reform Act of 1986 S corporations are required to recognize gain at the corporate level is not a disincentive to conversion, since the amount of the recognized gain increases the shareholder's basis for the stock thereby decreasing the shareholder's gain on liquidation (i.e., there is still just a single tax, compared to the double taxation levied on regular (C) corporations.) Congress thus provided that new Section 1374 would apply where a regular (C) corporation had converted to S corporation status if the election took place after 1986 and the corporation subject to tax had a recognized built-in gain during the ten-year period following the first day of its first S corporation year.

The tax is imposed at the highest corporate rate and applies to the lesser of the recognized built-in gain for the year or to the amount that would be the taxable income of the corporation were it a regular (C) corporation for the year.

To find the recognized built-in gain subject to tax you take the lowest of the following: (1) the entire recognized gain; (2) the amount of the built-in gain on the first S corporation day with respect to the property sold; or (3) the net unrealized built-in gain on the first S corporation day minus the recognized built-in gains in prior years during the ten-year period. (The tax is applicable to the proceeds of any "disposition" of assets made during such period. Disposition means any sale or distribution, whether or not in the course of liquidation, as well as the collection of accounts receivable and the completion of contracts under the completed contract method.)

For example, assume a regular (C) corporation elects S corporation status on February 2, 1991. Under federal tax law, if any S corporation is to be effective for a corporation's existing tax year, Form 2553 must be filed no later than the fifteenth day of the third month of the corporation's taxable year. In the case of an existing corporation (as here) wishing to convert to S corporation status, an election must be made by March 15 to be effective for the current year; an election made after that date would be effective beginning with the following tax year.

In this case, the corporation made a timely election. Its first day as an S corporation is January 1, 1991 at which time, for the sake of simplicity, assume it held just two assets, one with a tax basis of $20,000 and an FMV of $60,000, the other with a tax basis of $20,000 and an FMV of $10,000. The corporation's total bases in the assets therefore is $40,000 while the total FMV of the assets is $70,000. This means that the net built-in gain for the assets on the corporation's first day as an S corporation is $30,000.

Now, assume that in 1991, the first asset is sold for $70,000. The built-in gain recognized for federal tax purposed is the lowest of three numbers: (1) the recognized gain, here, $70,000 minus $20,000, or $50,000; (2) the built-in gain at January 1, 1991, here, $60,000 FMV minus $20,000 tax basis, or $40,000; or (3) the net unrealized built-in gain on January 1, 1991, less the recognized built-in gains in prior S corporation years during the ten-year period, here, $60,000 minus $0, or $60,000. The lowest of the three is $40,000, which is the amount of gain that must be recognized in 1991 for federal tax purposes. Assuming an applicable tax rate of 34 percent, the tax to the corporation will be $13,600. This means that of the total recognized capital gain of $50,000, the corporation must pay tax on just the $40,000 allowing more gain to pass through to the shareholder. In this case, the pass-through is $50,000 minus $13,600 or $36,400, on which the shareholder would pay individual tax. The shareholder's basis for the stock in the corporation would be increased by $36,400, the amount of the pass-through.

141

Since the taxpayer must be able to show the original built-in gain on the first day the corporation became an S corporation on an asset-by-asset basis, an appraisal must be made. In fact, without proof of the original built-in gain, the entire gain is treated as recognized built-in gain.

In sum, an S corporation, unlike a regular (C) corporation, is generally not subject to tax at the corporate level, although shareholders are subject to tax on the pass-through. However, there are exceptions to this rule, the one discussed here concerns the so-called built-in gains. In order to prevent the conversion of eligible (C) corporations to S corporation status to avoid the tax effects of the repeal of the *General Utilities* doctrine, a corporate-level built-in gains tax is imposed on any gain that arose prior to the conversion and is recognized by the S corporation within ten years after the effective date of the S corporation election. For this purpose, a built-in gain is the excess of an asset's FMV on the date the election became effective over the corporation's adjusted basis in the asset on such date. This law applies only to tax years beginning after December 31, 1986, and even if it made its S corporation election after December 31, 1986, only if the S corporation was previously a regular (C) corporation; it does not apply to newly formed corporations that elect S corporation status. A different Section 1374, now known as old Section 1374, imposed a corporate-level capital gains tax if certain conditions were met. This statute does not apply if a corporation is subject to new Section 1374.

Since S corporations are now subject to a corporate level tax on built-in gains, those contemplating the eventual sale of a business may wish to minimize the tax effect of future appreciation of such assets by making an immediate S corporation election to cap the gains that must be recognized, taking care to have appraisals taken as of the first day of the S corporation year.

40

TAXATION OF
START-UP COSTS

Whether you plan to form a proprietorship, partnership, or corporation, you'll undoubtedly incur start-up expenses. This key discusses the federal tax treatment of start-up costs incurred in all three forms.

The general rule for proprietorships is that start-up expenses may be amortized over a period of not less than 60 months if a proper election is made by attaching a statement of election to the tax return for the first tax year. Without a proper election, no deduction is allowed. The rationale for this law is that although organizational costs are not deductible when they are paid, since they are associated with the creation of a capital asset, the actual period of the write-off that should be allowed is unclear since such costs benefit the entity over its entire useful life. The 60-month period is considered to be a reasonable compromise.

Start-up expenses include those costs incurred in connection with investigating and creating a business activity prior to the time the business activity begins operation. To determine whether an item is truly a start-up expense or is an operating expense (and thus currently deductible), you must look to the time the cost was incurred. Although it is impossible to develop an exhaustive list of such costs, they can generally be divided into investigative, organizational, and pre-opening expenses.

Typical of the first category is a payment to a business consultant. The second category includes expenses such as accounting and legal costs and payments made to state agencies. The third category includes such items as loan commitment fees and guarantee fees.

Most costs incurred in organizing a partnership receive

similar tax treatment to the proprietorship, and are capitalized and amortized over a period of not less than 60 months, beginning in the month in which the partnership begins doing business. Syndication costs incurred in selling partnership interests, such as accounting, printing, and legal costs, must be capitalized and can never be amortized; thus, it is better for a cost to be characterized as an organizational cost rather than as a syndication cost. The IRS may take the position that fees paid to promoters and similar up-front fees are organizational in nature and must be amortized. As with a proprietorship, if the election was not made on the partnership's first tax return, the opportunity may be lost.

The law related to corporations is similar in tax treatment to the proprietorship and the partnership. Organizational costs are amortizable at the election of the corporation over a period of not less than 60 months, beginning with the month in which the corporation begins doing business. The election to amortize them is binding on all subsequent years, and the length of the amortization period cannot be changed. However, if the corporation is dissolved, any unamortized organizational costs are fully deductible.

The amortization begins the month the corporation begins doing business, which is not necessarily the same time as when corporate existence begins. The reason is that corporate existence generally begins when the articles of incorporation are filed with the secretary of state's office, although, subject to state law, a different date may be specified; that is not necessarily the same time the corporation begins doing business (starts performing the operations for which it was created).

An organizational cost is one that is incidental to the creation of the corporation, is chargeable to the corporation's capital account, and is of a character that, if it were expended incident to the creation of a corporation having a limited life, would be amortizable over such limited life. Organizational costs include fees for legal and accounting services incurred in forming the corporation, fees paid to the state, and expenses of temporary directors and organizational meetings. Costs related to the issuance of stock, such as printing costs and underwriters' commissions, are neither amortizable nor deductible. Such costs reduce the shareholders' equity since they are treated as a reduction in the proceeds from the sale of stock.

The treatment of start-up costs is similar to that of organizational costs, and an election to amortize such costs over a period of not less than 60 months beginning with the month the corporation begins doing business must be made when the first tax return is filed. Again, the election must be made in the first tax return regardless of when the expenses are actually paid; any unamortized start-up costs are fully deductible if the business is terminated.

Proprietors and members of partnerships are well advised to incorporate at least initially in order to ensure that investigative and preopening expenses will be deductible should the venture prove unsuccessful and be terminated; such costs if incurred by noncorporate entities that are not engaged in a trade or business are never deductible since such costs are personal in nature. If the business is successful, the corporation can operate; if it proves unsuccessful, the shareholders will be allowed an ordinary loss deduction, assuming the stock qualifies as Section 1244 stock. Although a loss incurred upon the disposition of stock is ordinarily subject to capital loss treatment and thus the amount of the loss is limited to the amount of capital gains incurred during the tax year plus $3,000, under Section 1244, single taxpayers are allowed to deduct as an ordinary loss up to the sum of $50,000 ($100,000 for married taxpayers filing joint returns), with any excess treated as a capital loss.

41

SECURITIES LAW CONSIDERATIONS

Although the subject of securities regulation is a complex one, the potential buyer or seller of a business should have at least an understanding of the fundamentals.

Generally, securities law considerations become relevant if a purchaser issues or transfers securities to the seller in payment of all or part of the purchase price or if the seller transfers securities to the purchaser. If securities are transferred for a valuable consideration, the transaction becomes subject to the anti-fraud provisions of federal and state securities law, where applicable, and appropriate disclosure must be made.

On the federal side, as a rule, instruments considered to be securities are subject to the federal securities laws if they are offered or sold in interstate commerce or through the mails. The Securities Act of 1933 applies to the original distribution and, in limited cases, to a secondary distribution of securities. The fundamental purpose of this law is to compel full public disclosure of all information material to an investor's ability to determine the real value of a security; a secondary purpose is to prevent fraud and misrepresentation in the interstate offer or sale of securities.

The Securities Exchange Act of 1934 also applies to securities sold in interstate commerce or through the mails. This law has a much broader scope than the Securities Act of 1933 and regulates a wide variety of securities matters, including registration and reporting requirements of listed and over-the-counter securities, proxy solicitation, margin trading, and the registration of securities exchanges, broker-dealers, and securities associations.

The state blue sky laws, which regulate the original distribution of securities within a state, vary but generally prohibit fraud in connection with the purchase or sale of securities and require the registration of brokers/dealers in securities. Some states require the filing of detailed information similar to that required by the 1933 Act for registration statements. Private actions to enforce the blue sky laws and the 1933 Act are generally permitted in addition to enforcement action by the state and the SEC.

For some time, many securities law specialists believed that the securities laws did not apply to the transfer of shares of stock if the purpose was to transfer the ownership of a business, reasoning that although shares of stock may have been involved, the transfer was in reality a means of conveying ownership. However, this so-called sale of business doctrine has been rejected by the U.S. Supreme Court and presumably will be rejected by state courts. In its decision, the Supreme Court held that the economic substance of a transaction is not a relevant consideration as long as the transaction involved is a transfer of what has the normal characteristics of stock. Since the 1933 Act applies to such sales, the usual disclosure standards of that Act pertain. The practical effect of the decision is twofold. First, the case creates a federal cause of action for securities fraud and makes available the rescission and restitution remedies provided by the 1933 Act in connection with the sale of a business made by the sale of stock. Second, the case reads the material misstatement or omission language into the representation and warranties provisions of every stock purchase contract. Thus, in addition to having a state cause of action for fraud, a defrauded purchaser can now sue in federal court. Sellers are well advised to study carefully the representations they make and to make full and frank disclosures about the business they are selling.

Sellers should contact their attorneys to determine if an exemption from the registration requirements is available for the planned transaction under federal and state law. If, for example, the stock issuance qualifies as a private placement (i.e., one not made to the public), registration is not required. Note that whether a given offering is "private" and thus exempt from registration is a question of fact, with the burden of proof on the party claiming the exemption. Note further that even where all exemption requirements are satisfied and even where the issue is exempt from registration, the anti-fraud provisions may apply, including the imposition of possible criminal sanctions.

42

REPRESENTATIONS AND LITIGATION

Once a business is bought and operations commence, the buyer frequently begins to express disappointment over one or more issues. For example, the seller may have represented that the inventory being conveyed is salable and fit for its intended use and free of any material defects in workmanship. The buyer may discover, however, that some of the inventory is not of salable quality at all.

In such a case, the assistance of an experienced attorney might have provided protection. Beyond the boilerplate representations contained in most asset sales, the buyer should have insisted on representations specifically tailored to the needs of the particular situation, including a warranty that all of the representations being made were true and correct and that, in the event of a breach of any representation, warranty, or covenant, the seller would indemnify and hold the buyer harmless from any cost, liability, or expense that might ensue. As additional protection, if the deal is seller-financed, the buyer should have been given the express right to offset such costs against the money payable to the seller under the agreement. There are other ways to protect the buyer as well; for instance, the buyer should have attempted to have some portion of the sales price escrowed for a period of time as security in case undisclosed liabilities were subsequently discovered.

What happens, though, if you as the buyer find you have been defrauded? In the context of a sale of stock, you can file suit under the federal, and perhaps a state, securities law. There are also common law remedies available in connection with both stock and asset sales.

With the merger of law and equity in most courts, you can generally plead both law and equity claims in the same action. Further, inconsistent counts may be alleged to preserve your rights (e.g., you can plead intentional infliction of emotional distress in one court and negligent infliction of emotional distress in the next).

Although other counts are possible, this key focuses on allegations of breach of warranty and fraud. In alleging a breach of warranty, which is also a breach of the contract itself, the plaintiff shows that the particular condition contained in the representations, warranties, or covenants made by the seller did not exist or was untrue. For example, most sales agreements contain a representation stating that there are no actions, suits, or proceedings pending or, to the seller's knowledge, threatened against or involving the seller or brought by the seller or affecting any of the purchased property. This means that if it is subsequently discovered that the seller had been served with a lawsuit alleging the manufacture of defective products, for example, the plaintiff can allege that the seller should have stated that the representation was true "other than" or "with the exception of" the products liability claim.

Damages in breach of warranty actions vary from state to state. Some states apply a "benefit-of-the-bargain" standard, meaning you can recover the difference between the value of the business as represented and the value as it actually existed on the sales date; other states apply an out-of-pocket standard, meaning you can recover only the difference between the price paid and the true value of the business on the sales date. Other states allow an election of remedies; generally the benefit-of-the-bargain standard is more advantageous to the purchaser. In addition to direct damages, consequential damages may be available. In any case, you can seek to rescind the contract itself.

To prove fraud, the plaintiff must show either the existence of an untrue representation, knowingly made, that was material to the value of the business or a knowing concealment of a material fact. Knowledge can be either actual or constructive (that is, the seller can be held responsible for what he or she should have known). Some sales involve both a breach of warranty and fraud. For example, if the seller represents that all merchandise is of merchantable, salable quality and it turns out that virtually all of it is obsolete, the buyer may have a valid claim on both bases. Although litigation is not the hoped-for end result, it is good practice not only to tailor the representations to one's particular case but to monitor and document compliance carefully with those representations. This will help if it becomes necessary to prove your case later on.

43

PROFESSIONAL ADVISERS

Most likely, you are going to need professional help with your business purchase. Initially, you will need to speak with an attorney, preferably one with expertise in small businesses. Your attorney will be able to assist you not only in checking out the business and preparing an agreement and related instruments, but in incorporating the new business, obtaining the necessary licenses, and getting the business going.

Next, you will need to consult with an accountant, preferably a CPA, certainly one with special expertise in dealing with small businesses. The accountant will be able to assist you in evaluating the numbers provided by the seller, deciding whether your financial position makes meeting the initial investment and subsequent financial demands feasible, whether you will likely be able to obtain other financing, tax matters, and similar pre-acquisition issues. Once you decide to buy, your accountant will be able to help you set up your bookkeeping system and to satisfy federal, state, and local tax requirements.

Next, you will need to speak with an insurance professional who can meet your business insurance needs, a real estate professional who can help you get the best possible lease and who is experienced in site selection and similar issues, and experts in investment and financial planning who are familiar with the valuation and role of small businesses. Aside from these compensated advisers, you will need a bank contact, preferably a branch manager. Ideally, you should conduct all of your banking in one bank, so that when you need to borrow funds, your banker will be familiar with your situation. Even if he or she should leave the bank or be transferred elsewhere, at least you'll have a track record at that bank and at that branch. Further, your banker may be able to help in the initial information-gathering process and be able to give you information regarding the best place to locate, when to open your new business, and other critical decisions.

How should you select your professional advisers? There are a number of techniques available. You should speak with your family, friends, other entrepreneurs, and especially those in a similar business. The professionals you deal with should be comfortable with each other and not feel that they are in competition with each other for your services; for example, preparing minutes of the annual shareholders and directors meetings is legal work and should be done only by an attorney. You should interview each professional before making a commitment; some offer a free initial consultation, while others charge their regular fee. You should feel free to interview several potential advisers and to query their background and expertise in the field before making a decision.

Of course, you should fully understand the basis for any fee to be charged. Accountants may quote a monthly fee; it is important to determine what that fee includes. Attorneys typically charge on a time basis, although certain types of services, such as incorporating a business, may be performed for a flat fee, and other types of services, such as collections work, may be done on a contingency-fee basis.

Be sure to understand what is included in your attorney's fee, too. For example, does preparing your incorporation include help in completing the applications for an employer identification number (IRS Form SS-4) and for the S corporation election (IRS Form 2553) both of which are simple to complete but very important. Fees are competitive, and it is worth checking around; some attorneys offer a form of package arrangement geared to small businesses. However, price should not be the sole, or even necessarily a major, criterion when you choose your advisers. You should be comfortable with them, with their professional qualifications, and with their commitment to your business and your industry. In the end, their competence and interest in meeting your needs will be vital to the success of your business as it grows.

QUESTIONS AND ANSWERS

What are the non-tax advantages of the corporate form?

The shareholder limits his liability to his investment in the business, although bankers and other lenders may require the shareholders to pledge their personal assets as security for corporate borrowings. The shareholder can more easily transfer his ownership interest. The corporation generally has a perpetual life—the death of the shareholder will not terminate corporate existence. It is relatively easy to raise capital. Banks, for example, are very familiar with the instruments issued by corporations.

What is the basic tax difference between operating as a proprietorship, a partnership, or a regular (C) corporation?

A proprietorship is not taxable as a separate entity and thus all of the tax effects are borne by the proprietor and reported on Schedule C, attached to the Form 1040. A partnership is not treated as a taxpayer but as a tax-reporting entity via Form 1065, with items of income, loss, deduction, and credit passed through to the partners. As an example, consider tax-exempt income, which, if distributed to the partners, retains its tax-exempt status in the hands of the partners. In a regular (C) corporation, such income will only retain its tax-exempt status at the corporate level. A regular (C) corporation is treated as a separate taxpayer and not just as a conduit, resulting in double taxation. First, there is a tax at the corporate level on the corporation's earnings; second, there is a tax at the shareholder level on the corporate after-tax income which is distributed to the shareholders as dividends.

A regular (C) corporation with one shareholder/employee has pre-tax income of $100,000 and is in the 34% tax bracket. The owner, who is in the 28% tax bracket, wishes to take as much after-tax income as possible out of the corporation. Corporate tax brackets are as follows:

$50,000 or less	15%
$50,000–75,000	25%
$75,000–$100,000	34%

If the corporation distributes all of its after-tax income to the owner as a dividend, how much will the owner have remaining after paying individual income taxes on the dividend?

The corporate tax on $100,000 is $22,250 leaving $77,750 of after-tax income. Since the shareholder is in the 28% tax bracket, the tax on $77,750 is $21,770. This means that the total taxes paid on the $100,000, assuming a 100% dividend, would be $44,020. This illustrates the problem of double taxation; first, the corporation pays tax on the earnings and then the shareholder pays tax on the dividend. As will be seen below, however, there are measures that can be taken, such as paying the shareholder-employee a salary, to minimize or avoid this problem.

If the corporation distributes $100,000 to the shareholder/employee as a salary, how much will the owner pay in taxes?

Assuming that the salary is a reasonable one, there is no corporate-level tax (i.e., corporate taxable income has been reduced to zero). The shareholder would pay $28,000 of tax on the $100,000 of salary.

Since the tax law only allows the employer a deduction for reasonable compensation, how do you determine what is reasonable?

In the normal case, you negotiate your compensation

with your employer, so the compensation level is likely to be respected. However, in the case of small, closely-held corporations, the IRS is more likely to challenge a salary as excessive and try to recharacterize deductible salary as a non-deductible dividend. To determine what is reasonable compensation, you consider not only the regular salary, but all overtime, bonuses, commissions, and fringe benefits received. A number of factors are considered to determine if a particular shareholder/employee's salary is excessive, such as the time devoted to the business, job qualifications, comparable salaries in the industry, and past services rendered.

Assuming that the corporation distributes all of its after-tax income to the shareholder/employee as a loan, what will be the tax effect?

The corporation would pay $22,250 of tax on the $100,000, leaving $77,750 to be loaned to the shareholder/employee at a reasonable rate of interest. The taxpayer would pay no taxes on the loan, meaning that the entire $77,750 is available after taxes. Years ago, some taxpayers tried to borrow funds on a zero-interest or low-interest basis. Due to a change in the tax law, however, this will lead to the imputation of income, and, further, the IRS may try to recharacterize the loan itself as a constructive dividend. It turns out that in the case of a regular (C) corporation, it is better to borrow from a qualified plan. For such a loan to be approved however, the loan provision needs to be approved, and the loans must be made available to all participants and beneficiaries on a reasonably equivalent basis, must not be available disproportionately to highly paid employees, officers, or shareholders, must be made pursuant to specific provisions regarding such loans as provided in the plan, must bear a reasonable rate of interest, and must be adequately secured. For this purpose, the vested portion in the plan participant's account can be used as security for the loan.

What is an S corporation?

A corporation automatically becomes a regular (C) corporation when it is formed; no special action need be taken. However, if the corporation, with the consent of the shareholders, makes an election to operate as an S corporation, the corporation will itself generally pay no taxes. Rather, the corporation's income, deductions, losses, and credits will flow through to the shareholders who report such items on their individual tax returns. This means that income is only taxed at the shareholder level. Generally, an individual owner's share of an item is calculated by taking the annual amount of the item and multiplying it by the owner's percentage interest in the stock of the corporation. This means that if a taxpayer owns 95 percent of an S corporation that has a $100,000, profit for the tax year, the taxpayer's share of the income would be $95,000. Note however that the income is taxed to the shareholder at his highest marginal rate. For example, if $10,000 of income were reported, the shareholder would be taxed on $9500 of income, not at the corporation's tax rate of 15 percent but at the higher individual tax bracket of 28 percent. The election must be filed on or before the fifteenth day of the third month of the corporation's taxable year. If the election is filed late, it will not be deemed effective until the following year. For a corporation to qualify for S corporation status, a number of criteria must be met: the corporation must be a U.S. corporation; none of the shareholders may be nonresident aliens; there may be only one class of stock, although differences in voting rights are permitted; all shareholders must be individuals, estates, or certain trusts; there must be no more than 35 shareholders; and the corporation cannot be a member of a group of affiliated corporations.

Is it ever a good idea to terminate the S corporation election?

As a general rule, once an S corporation becomes profitable, the shareholder will be better off terminating the S corporation election and becoming a regular (C) corporation, unless the S corporation is distributing all of its income to the shareholders as earned. The reason is that a profitable regular (C) corporation takes dollars off the top of the shareholder/employee's personal tax liability; the exact amount of earnings to be left in the corporation is fairly flexible since the shareholder/employee is ordinarily drawing a tax-deductible salary, and further there are other means—such as fringe benefits—that can avoid having a payment characterized as a nondeductible dividend. A well-established way is through the implementation of a comprehensive fringe benefit program.

Name some tax-deductible fringe benefits that can be provided tax-free to a shareholder/employee but need not be provided to substantially all full-time employees on a nondiscriminatory basis.

Disability insurance
Free meals and housing on company premises
Free parking
Medical examinations
Payment of professional and business club dues
Subscriptions to business publications
De minimis fringe benefits.

Name some tax-deductible fringe benefits that can be provided tax-free to a shareholder/employee but must be provided to substantially all full-time employees on a nondiscriminatory basis.

$50,000 of group-term life insurance
Tuition reimbursement plans
Medical and dental insurance and medical reimbursement plans
Pensions or profit-sharing plans
Child and dependent care, subject to limitations
Recreational and health facilities.

What is the function of "basis"?

Basis is primarily used in measuring the amount of gain or loss realized on the sale, exchange, or other disposition of property. It is also used for such purposes as the determination of the amount of depreciation or amortization allowable an asset. Several methods are used in determining one's initial basis. Generally, a taxpayer's initial basis in an asset will equal the cost of the asset ("cost basis"). Thus, if you spend $10,000 for a piece of machinery, your initial basis in the machinery is $10,000. In certain cases, a taxpayer's initial basis is established by reference to somebody else's basis ("carryover basis"). As an example, if property is received by gift, generally, the donee will take the donor's basis. In other cases, a taxpayer's basis in one asset may be transferred to another asset owned by the taxpayer ("substituted basis"). As an example of substituted basis, a partner's basis in his partnership interest includes his basis in the property he contributed to the business. As an example of carryover basis, the partnership's basis in property contributed to it generally equals the contributing partner's basis in that property. Regardless of the method used to determine initial basis, said amount will be increased or decreased to record subsequent events having a tax effect. To continue the prior example, if that machinery is depreciated on a straight-line basis over a ten-year period, then, assuming no salvage value, the annual depreciation deduction would be $1000, and the corporation's adjusted basis after the first year would be $9000.

What is a shareholder's initial basis in his stock?

The initial basis includes cash and the basis of any property contributed to the corporation as well as the amount of any gain recognized when the property was contributed to the corporation. Thus, if you contribute $10,000 to the ABC corporation in consideration for the issuance of 100 shares of common stock, your tax basis in the shares is $10,000. If two years later, the shares are sold for $100,000, your tax basis in the shares is still $10,000, and your gain on the sale would be $90,000.

What are the tax consequences of forming a corporation?

Generally, a gain or loss is recognized when an asset is exchanged. However, Section 351 is an important exception to this rule and, when the requirements are met, mandates that no gain or loss need be recognized on corporate formation, and that the basis of the transferred property carry over to the transferee corporation with the transferor having the same basis in the stock or securities that he receives as he had in the transferred property. For Section 351 to apply, the following requirements must be met: there must be a transfer of property to the corporation (such property includes money, machinery, buildings, land, and similar items and also includes patents, leases, secret processes and other forms of know-how, but does not include services, past, present, or future); the property must be transferred solely in exchange for stock or securities of the corporation (such stock can be common, preferred, voting or non-voting, but not stock rights, warrants, options or convertible bonds, while such securities may include long-term debt, that is, with at least five years left to maturity); and the person or group of persons who transferred the property must have control of the corporation immediately after the exchange (the term "person" includes all entities legally treated as such meaning individuals, corporations, partnerships, trusts and estates while the term "control" means ownership of at least 80% of the combined voting power of all classes of stock entitled to vote and at least 80% of the total number of shares of all other classes of stock and the term "immediately after the exchange" means an orderly execution of a previously defined agreement but does not necessarily require a simultaneous exchange).

What happens if a transferor receives only securities in the exchange?

Each person transferring assets to the corporation must have an equity interest in the new corporation and hence an exchange in which a transferor only receives securities will not qualify.

Does Section 351 work with a post-incorporation transfer?

Yes. A post-incorporation transfer can be treated as a Section 351 tax-free exchange so long as the transferors receive stock or securities in the corporation and, as a group, they control the corporation immediately after the transfer. Note though that if a transfer of assets in exchange for stock or securities does not qualify under Section 351, it will be treated as a sale with the transferor required to recognize any gain or loss on the transfer. Of course, if the transfer doesn't receive anything at all in the exchange, the transaction is simply treated as a contribution to the capital of the corporation and a tax-free increase in the corporation's capital.

Aren't there exceptions to this rule regarding tax-free incorporation?

Yes. There are three major exceptions. The first exception is known as the "boot" exception. The second exception is called the liabilities in excess of basis exception. The third exception is called the services exception.

What is the "boot" exception?

A contribution of property to a corporation will be tax-free only if the person contributing property receives stock or long-term debt obligations of the corporation in exchange. If other property is received "to boot," the property transferred will be partly or fully taxable depending on the fair market value of the boot received. For example, if you transfer $10,000 for 100 shares of a newly formed corporation, your basis in the shares will be $10,000 and no gain is recognized. If you transfer equipment with a fair market value of $10,000 and a tax basis of $1,000 for 100 shares of a newly-formed corporation, your tax basis will be $1,000 in the shares and none of the $9000 gain will be immediately recognized. However, if you make the same transfer but receive say 50 shares and $5,000 of short-term debt, you have received property other than stock or long-term debt ("boot") in the amount of $5,000, which means that $5000 of the $9000 gain must be recognized. Regardless of the amount of boot received in an exchange, you recognize only the lesser of the FMV of the boot received in the exchange or the realized gain (here, the lesser of $5000 or $9000).

What is the character of the income from the boot?

The character of the income the shareholders must report when they receive boot depends on the kind of assets being transferred. Thus, if a sale of an asset would have produced capital gain, the boot income is capital gain, but if a sale of the asset would have produced ordinary income, the boot income is treated as ordinary income.

What is the tax effect of "boot" on basis?

If the transferor receives only stock or securities from the transferee corporation, the basis in the shares is the same as the basis in the transferred property, but if boot is received by the transferor in addition, the basis of the stock or securities will equal the basis of the transferred property plus any gain recognized by the transferor on the exchange minus the cash or the FMV of the boot received. The transferee's basis in the property received meanwhile will be the same as the transferor's basis plus any gain recognized by the transferor as a result of the exchange.

Explain the liabilities in excess of basis exception.

Generally, a corporation's assumption of a liability—or its acquisition of an asset subject to a liability—will neither disqualify the transaction from tax-free status nor produce taxable income to the shareholders (i.e., it is *not* considered to be boot). Although the corporation will take a carryover basis in the property, the transferor's basis in the stock is decreased by the amount of the liability assumed. However, if a transfer is motivated by tax avoidance or the corporation does not have a bona fide business purpose for assuming a liability, the corporation's assumption of a liability, or its acquisition of an asset subject to a liability, will be treated as boot. For example, if you contribute property encumbered by a $30,000 mortgage to the ABC corporation in exchange for 100 shares of common stock, and your tax basis in the property is $20,000, your taxable income resulting from the contribution would be $10,000. This determination is made on a shareholder by shareholder basis with all of the assets and liabilities transferred by each shareholder aggregated to make the finding.

Explain the services exception.

Stock received for services performed for a corporation does not qualify as property and therefore is treated as compensation to the transferor. Moreover, a recipient of stock issued solely for services to be performed, or already performed, does not count for purposes of satisfying the 80% test. Note that if both property is transferred and services are performed by a transferor however, all of the stock that person receives for the assets and services is considered in determining whether the control test has been met.

Are there times when it might be better for an incorporation to be taxable?

Yes. There may be times when it is desirable to avoid the application of Section 351 and for the transfer to be treated as a taxable event (i.e., a taxable sale.) In such case, the transferee-corporation will take a higher basis in the property—a basis equal to the FMV of the property. The transferor will recognize gain and therefore ordinarily have a lower taxable gain on the later disposition of the stock. Examples of situations warranting such treatment are the following: the transferor has unused net operating losses and can use the carryover to offset the gain from the incorporation; an asset with a built-in loss is transferred to the corporation (although Section 351 doesn't permit loss recognition, making the exchange a taxable event will generally permit the transferor to recognize the loss immediately); and a taxable sale could result in the ability to achieve a higher basis if the acquiring corporation makes a Section 338 election when it acquires a subsidiary (as discussed in this book, with the passage of the Tax Reform Act of 1986, a Section 338 election is ordinarily inadvisable other than with respect to the acquisition of a subsidiary from a consolidated group as set forth in Section 338(h)(10)). Note: there are various ways to disqualify an exchange and make a transfer taxable such as by deliberately failing the control test.

What is the tax effect of a corporation suffering losses?

It is common for a start-up enterprise to incur losses in the early years. If a regular (C) corporation is used, such losses will result in no tax benefit to the individual shareholders since the losses belong to the corporation. Had the S corporation election been in effect however, such losses would pass through to the respective shareholders and be deductible by them against their other income. Further, if stock qualifies as "Section 1244" stock and becomes worthless, the stock qualifies as an ordinary loss to the extent of $50,000 for a single taxpayer and $100,000 for a married taxpayer filing a joint return. This is the case whether the corporation was a regular (C) corporation or an S corporation. (Note: Section 1244 stock is common or preferred stock issued in exchange for cash or property other than stock or securities of the issuer or another company; at the time of issuance, the aggregate amount of money and property that the corporation has received must not exceed $1 million).

If a regular (C) corporation has earnings and profits, how is a corporate distribution to the shareholders taxed?

If a regular (C) corporation has earnings and profits (E & P), a distribution of cash or property will be fully taxable to the recipient as a dividend. Once E & P has been reduced to zero however, such distributions will be tax free until the shareholder receives an amount equal to one's basis in the shares, and thus the basis has been reduced to zero. Thereafter, any distributions will be taxed as capital gain. For example, assume that you own 100 shares of the ABC corporation with a tax basis of $10,000 and the corporation has E & P of $10,000. For the current tax year, the corporation makes a distribution of $25,000. The distribution is taxable to you as follows: the first $10,000 is taxable as a dividend, the next $10,000 reduces your basis in your shares down to $0, and the next $5000 is taxable to you as a capital gain. (Note: the rules are somewhat different for an S corporation with E & P).

I want to form an S corporation. I understand preferred stock is not permitted in the capital structure, but what about debt?

Debt could be an alternative. As mentioned previously, distributions to shareholders are nondeductible; however, loans made by the shareholders generally result in tax-deductible interest. With that in mind, many corporations are motivated to an excessive level of debt vs. equity and risk IRS recharacterization of the debt as equity and the interest payments as dividends. The IRS looks at a number of factors to determine if an obligation is really debt. First, there should be a note, which is an unqualified promise to pay principal and interest. The obligation should be treated as such not just on the tax returns but in all of the corporate financial and other records. The debt should have a fixed maturity date and if the debt is to be paid in installments, a definite repayment plan should exist and be followed. The corporation must be required to pay a reasonable rate of interest and the rate (and payments) should not hinge on corporate earnings. Second, the shareholder-creditor should be able to enforce the debt, the debt should not be convertible into stock, and the shareholder debt should not be subordinated to that of a bank or other commercial lender. Although a bank or other lender would understandably wish to subordinate such a debt, such a practice is inherently suspect to the IRS. Relatedly, debt issued proportionately to share ownership in a company is more likely to look like equity. Thus, if two shareholders each own 50 percent of the capital and 50 percent of the debt, this proportionality of interest leads to a finding of equity. Further, the IRS will look to the debt/equity ratio. For this purpose, both inside debt (debt owed to shareholders) and outside debt (debt owed to outside parties) will be included in the debt figure, so that a thinly capitalized business (i.e., one with a high debt/equity ratio) is more likely to have its so-called debt recharacterized as additional equity. In sum, a good test to remember is whether an independent creditor would have made the loan to the corporation under similar circumstances. If so, recharacterization of the debt as equity is less likely.

GLOSSARY

assignment A transfer of property or some interest therein from one person to another. The transferor is known as the assignor; the other original party to the contract is known as the obligor, and the transferee is known as the assignee.

bulk sales act State laws intended to protect the creditors of a business which is being sold by requiring that they be notified of the sale. Compliance with the law can cause delay and expense since various documents have to be completed and no action can be taken until the statutory waiting periods have elapsed.

closely-held corporations Such corporations are characterized by few shareholders, most of whom are actively involved in the management of the business either as an employee or officer, and there exists little, if any, market for their shares.

condition A provision in a contract which can rescind or suspend the principal obligation.

condition precedent A condition which must occur before either party is bound by the principal obligation of a contract.

condition subsequent A condition which operates to discharge one from his or her obligations under a contract.

convenant An agreement concerning acts which one will or will not perform.

gross profit margin The corporation's gross profit as a percentage of sales (i.e., profit after deducting the cost of goods sold).

leverage The use of borrowed funds to magnify a gain or loss on the principal amount involved.

note A promise to pay unconditionally a certain sum

168

of money at a certain date, whether on demand or at some specific date.

novation A mutual agreement, between all parties involved, for the discharge of a validly existing obligation by the substitution of a new valid obligation on the part of the debtor or another, or a like agreement for the discharge of a debtor to his or her creditor by the substitution of a new creditor.

operating profit margin The corporation's operating profit as a percentage of sales (i.e., profit after deducting the cost of goods sold and operating costs).

point One percent of some principal amount. Loan origination charges are generally expressed as points of the amount of the borrowing. Thus, one point on a $100,000 loan amounts to $1,000. Paying points adds to the borrower's cost of capital.

price/earnings ratio The market value of a firm expressed as a multiple of its earnings for the most recent fiscal/calendar year or the past 12 months.

private placement In order to raise capital, one may make a sale of securities, through debt or stock, through direct negotiations with the purchasers. Such shares cannot be sold unless registered with the SEC, and the applicable jurisdiction, unless an exemption is available. In a private placement, the acquirer of such shares states his or her intent not to resell the shares publicly and thus the shares are known as "letter stock." Founders' shares not registered with the SEC are also referred to as letter stock.

public corporation A public corporation is one in which the ownership consists of widely separated holdings.

security agreement An agreement which creates or provides a security interest or lien on personal property.

undercapitalization An undercapitalized or a thinly capitalized company is one with a small equity investment by its shareholders, thus resulting in higher leverage—that is, a higher level of debt relative to equity.

warranty A warranty may apply to a present or future fact whereas a representation only applies to an existing fact.

INDEX